T0305308

The City and Quality of Life

CITIES SERIES

Series Editor: John Rennie Short, *Department of Public Policy, University of Maryland, Baltimore County, USA*

As we move into a more urban future, cities are the main setting for social change, economic transformations, political challenges and ecological concerns.

This series aims to capture some of the excitement and challenges of understanding cities. It provides a forum for interdisciplinary and transdisciplinary scholarship. International in scope, it will embrace empirical and theoretical studies, comparative and case study approaches. The series will provide a discussion site and theoretical platform for cutting edge research by publishing innovative and high quality authored, co-authored and edited works at the frontier of contemporary urban scholarship.

Titles in the series include:

The City and Quality of Life

Peter Karl Kresl

*Charles P. Vaughan Professor of Economics (Emeritus),
Bucknell University, USA and Co-founder and Past President,
Global Urban Competitiveness Project*

CITIES SERIES

 Edward **Elgar**
PUBLISHING

Cheltenham, UK • Northampton, MA, USA

Published by
Edward Elgar Publishing Limited
The Lypiatts
15 Lansdown Road
Cheltenham
Glos GL50 2JA
UK

Edward Elgar Publishing, Inc.
William Pratt House
9 Dewey Court
Northampton
Massachusetts 01060
USA

A catalogue record for this book
is available from the British Library

Library of Congress Control Number: 2021932433

This book is available electronically in the **Elgar**online
Economics subject collection
http://dx.doi.org/10.4337/9781800880115

ISBN 978 1 80088 010 8 (cased)
ISBN 978 1 80088 011 5 (eBook)

Printed and bound by CPI Group (UK) Ltd, Croydon, CR0 4YY

Contents

1. Introduction: the importance of the quality of urban life

Economies are usually in a state of change, with periods of secular stagnation being one exception to the rule. This evolution from an economy of one basic nature to that of another is presumably a movement to an economy that is better or more efficient, with enhanced productivity and increased availability of goods and services for the population. In the course of this evolution the economy becomes more complex, more technologically sophisticated, more dependent upon flexibility and adaptability to new circumstances. The past 150 years have been marked by the evolution from an economy of "blue collar" manufacturing in industrial concerns, or factories, with workers characterized by manual labor, often highly skilled, organized in unions, having little leisure time, and little life after the end of the working years. Workers often walked to their job, had little formal education, and anticipated that their children would follow in the steps of their parents.

In recent decades, the economy has changed to the detriment of these workers and their employment. Technology has made many of their skills no longer relevant to the contemporary mode of production, their children have gained some level of education that has opened other lines of work to them, the towns and cities in which they have spent their lives have become shadows of their former vitality, unions are declining in both membership and power, and inadequate policy response to the structural changes from increasing international trade has left them on the sidelines of the globalized economy. These deteriorating conditions had their first impact on the US African American population, and then a couple of decades later decimated the country's White population. In each instance, as Ann Case and Angus Deaton have detailed so well, the populations have been decimated by "deaths of despair", alcoholism, suicide, and drug use – heroin and crack cocaine with African Americans and then OxyContin with the White population a couple of decades later. (Case and Deaton, Part I) Economic progress has been decreasingly kind to workers who lack a university degree and the skill set that comes with it.

The most recent developments in the economy have seen a transition from manufacturing as the primary source of employment to the services sector, including financial services, retail, real estate, personal services, travel, hospitality, education, healthcare, and government, that is, from the Fordist to the post-Fordist economy. (Scott, pp. 6–11) This has been fed by the rapid development of robotics, computerization, advanced communications, and other transformations of the production of goods and services. As the coronavirus pandemic has demonstrated so dramatically, many workers no longer need a desk in an office tower, but can telecommute their work from home or almost anywhere. This is likely to have powerful and far-reaching implications for public and private transportation (including air travel), residential housing, the attractiveness of living in the city or in a suburb, the attractiveness of large cities versus smaller cities, the market for commercial space and office towers, the demand for education and other approaches to skill development, and almost every other aspect of modern living.

As is appropriate to this new stage in the development of the economy, the characteristics and preferences of the new labor force differ greatly from those of the previous generation of workers. Of fundamental importance is the fact that today's tech workers have a variety of options that were never available to yesterday's workers. Having a university education immediately enhances the worker's attractiveness to employers which leads to increased mobility, flexibility, and strength in the decision-making process. The worker can choose the location, nature, and characteristics of the employment that is decided. Younger workers have specific preferences for ambience, social life, and characteristics of the job, often they have young families and demand the appropriate education, public security, quality of neighborhood, public transportation, and amenities such as recreational and cultural offerings of the city or town chosen. Therefore, the educated worker has power in the market for labor that was rarely the case for the previous generation. These sought-after characteristics can be combined into what one can refer to as "quality of life", or QoL. In the words of Edward Glaeser: "People are increasingly choosing areas on the basis of quality of life, and the skilled people who come to attractive areas then provide the new ideas that fuel the local economy. Smart, entrepreneurial people are the ultimate source of a city's economic power, and as those people become more prosperous, they care more about quality of life." (Glaeser, p. 132)

In recent years increased attention has been given to the role of quality of life in various important aspects of a city's economy. In the earlier period many cities had distinct roles to play in the economy – Pittsburgh is where steel was produced, in Detroit it was automobiles, Seattle was aircraft, New York was finance and Chicago was the transportation gateway for the Mid-west agricultural economy to world markets. Many other cities have had distinctive roles since their earliest years. In the new economy, this has changed dramatically. Some economic activity has gone abroad to areas that are closer to markets or to low cost labor and production. However, while Detroit is still struggling to find its place, Chicago, Seattle, Pittsburgh and New York, along with many other cities, have found new roles for themselves in the new technology-based economy.

The new economy is a fluid economy with production evolving into new technologies and new products, with new cities entering the competitive scene and some cities being abandoned due to an inability to evolve quickly and suitably enough, and with firms being linked in global structures or networks. At the goods end of the process, cities are increasingly in competition with each other. Firms can be attracted to opportunities that are made available to them by other cities, firms are often merged into larger structures in which the original host city no longer has a role to play, and, of course, firms can become bankrupt. In all of these instances the city in question loses out, and either adapts to the new world or slowly deteriorates in relation to other cities. In this world of increased flux, cities must be constantly alert to challenges and opportunities, and must be proactive with regard to the evolution of their economy and its key actors.

Today's cities and the firms in their economy must also be aggressive when it comes to the key resource in that economy – the high skilled, highly mobile, and younger labor force. The workers in this labor force can choose the city in which they want to work and live, and can, indeed, opt to work for a firm in one city and to telecommute from a home in a rural location, or in any other place, distant from that city. What these workers seek is a quality of life that suits their needs and those of their family. In this labor market the power has shifted to a considerable degree from the employer to the employee. These are the firms that now make up the key element in the economy of a city that is playing in this field. Each city has to make itself attractive to these highly mobile workers by enhancing the quality of life elements that are important to them.

This is the central point of discussion for the book that follows. In it we will examine several principal aspects of the importance of quality of life for contemporary cities.

THE STRUCTURE OF THE BOOK

There are six aspects that will be elaborated on in the six chapters that follow. Each treats a distinct element in the complex that comprises "quality of life", from the standpoint of its relevance to urban economies. The first half of the book will examine the consequences of quality of life and the second will discuss the components of quality of life. That is to say, the first half will examine what quality of life can do for or to a city's economy, and in the second half we will discuss how a city can enhance its quality of life. This distinction between consequences and components is, of course, a bit artificial since the two sets of linkages blend into each other at points. Nonetheless, it is still useful to structure the elements in this way as this captures the principal aspects of the relationships as, I hope, will be clear by the end of the text.

The Consequences of Quality of Life

Having a high or low quality of life will have important consequences for the vitality and status of any city. This should be self-evident, but it is in the specifics that we find things that are of interest to us. The first issue we will discuss is that of "happiness", a concept that has come into prominence in urban studies in recent years. The second is the impact of quality of life on the competitiveness of the city. The third is its impact on important aspects of the economy itself.

Chapter 2 – contemporary analysis of quality of life

For most of the history of the study of economics, its practitioners have had little to say about quality of life, per se. From its earliest days, economists have recognized the contribution to human wellbeing of friendship, collegiality, good conversation, and other non-material aspects of social intercourse, but the problem arises when it is clear that none of this can be quantified, measured, and calculated. These elements slip through one's fingers and one is left with material goods and exchangeable services. Hence, we have searched in vain for much of a discussion of quality of life until rather recently. During the past decade economists have become intrigued by the notion of "happiness". Luigini Bruni gives us a very informative review of the development of the notion of "happiness" during the past two centuries. (Bruni) Indeed, we now have a Global Happiness Council that calculates annually a World Happiness Report. (Sustainable Development Solutions Network) At this point, it is sufficient to note that a questionnaire is distributed to residents in 157 countries, and the result is a ranking of countries from most to least happy. Other research entities have entered this area and have issued their own similar indices of something roughly approximating the concept of happiness.

At the level of the city, which is our primary concern, there are several approaches to study and promotion of "urban happiness". The mayor of Paris, Anne Hidalgo, has, earlier this year, introduced an initiative to create a "15 minute city", based on an advisor's notion that there are six things that make an urbanite happy and they are all centered on the notion that one should cluster the various elements in a resident's daily life to a smaller radius than is currently the case. (O'Sullivan) This leads into a policy approach that promotes bicycles instead of automobiles, and to promotion of other policies to reduce global warming. Promotion of urban happiness quickly leads one to a much broader set of policy initiatives.

Other economists have linked quality of life with amenities, the business climate, climate and environmental aspects, and diversity and inclusion. One found that 40 percent of the growth in college graduates in a city's labor force was attributable to increased quality of life. (Shapiro, p. 3) In a break with the work of orthodox economists, one set of analysts of the developing world found that many wealthy countries fail to achieve an acceptable level of wellbeing while this is achieved in many of the poorest countries. (McGregor, Camfield and Woodcock)

In all of these studies, one of the primary interests for this book is the set of variables the various authors have used to analyze or to measure quality of life.

Chapter 3 – quality of life and competitiveness

Competitiveness in relation to other cities has become an extremely important issue for the contemporary city and its leaders. With companies and skilled workers so mobile and willing to move from one city to another that offers whatever it is that they find desirable, no city can afford to rest on its past accomplishments and successes. The entire structure in which city, firm and worker exist today has a fluidity that has not been seen before. The study of this phenomenon, urban competitiveness, has attracted a large number of researchers since the 1990s and in their work several have included the role of quality of life in the enhancement of a city's competitiveness, some of which is discussed by Daniel Naud and Remy Tremblay, while noting some difficulty in its definition. (Naud and Tremblay)

Peter Karl Kresl and Balwant Singh have broken the determinants of competitiveness into two categories, hard and soft. (Kresl and Singh, pp. 244–5) Whereas the former are features such as location, a major airport, research labs, capital stock, and population growth, the soft determinants include public security, health facilities, recreation, congenial neighborhoods, and public education. Clearly, the soft determinants are more easily managed than are the hard ones. Quality of life per se tends to be composed of the soft determinants. In their study, Kresl and Singh found that, over time, the soft determinants have become more important as determinants of urban competitiveness than the harder ones. This conforms with the increased attention that is being given to quality of life in the study of urban competitiveness.

There is clearly a dynamic element to this in that the factors that make a city's quality of life attractive to firms and workers at one time may not be suitable a few years later. The city must continually evaluate its strengths and weaknesses in this regard and must be conscious of the need to modify its amenities and attributes over time. This in itself calls for an activist and engaged city government, and for responsive agencies and governance structures.

Chapter 4 – quality of life and the economy

Having a high or low quality of life will have a powerful impact on the nature of the city's economy. First is the structure of the economy. Having a good quality of life means that the city has choices in creating the sort of economy it seeks to have. It has options rather than being obligated to take whichever manufacturing and service sector firms choose to locate within its limits. In the latter case, it may be a firm that seeks only the lowest paid and skilled workers it can find for the low level activities it wants to develop. The city is then just a taker and is not able to be a demander in its economic development. The high quality of life city can actively market itself and can work to create an economy that is environmentally clean, actively growing over time, has a labor force that will be attracted to a lively retail, housing and amenity complex and that will seek on its own to enhance these elements to the city's milieu. This is evocative of Richard Florida's "Winner Take-All Urbanism". (Florida, ch. 2)

This can also be seen in the evolution of that economy over decades as one success works to build another success. With a poor quality of life, over time the city will deteriorate in several ways as talented workers seek employment elsewhere and desirable firms also decline or relocate. Once this deterioration begins, it is virtually impossible to turn it around except with the most vision-ary and effective leadership. Pittsburgh was able to make a transition from steel to medical technology and robotics, Chicago transitioned from basic steel to high alloy specialty steel, and many other cities with high quality of life have made similar transitions; others, such as Youngstown, have been less successful.

The final quality of life issue we will examine is the relationship between the city and the national economy and with other levels of government. Cities develop reputations among other cities and among an array of economic actors throughout the nation. When firms look for new places to establish entities they seek locations their employees will find to be congenial. When cities partner with other cities in any sort of initiative they look for places that will be trouble free and will make a contribution to the initiative. Cities that have a reputation for having a positive quality of life are attractive places for this sort of cooperation. They participate in what Bruce Katz and Jennifer Bradley refer to as participation in a "global network of trading cities". (Katz and Bradley, ch. 7) Troubled cities are not attractive partners to other cities. With reference to state and national governments, troubled cities tend to be drains on resources, while those cities with a high quality of life tend to seek funding for cultural, beautification, transportation and other initiatives that bring benefits to residents from other cities who are attracted to visit them.

The Components of Quality of Life

Cities vary considerably in their quality of life. We have just seen how important this can be for any city. What determines a city's quality of life? In this section we will examine what are arguably the three most powerful factors that enhance a city's quality of life. First is a set of demographic elements that treat the composition and the development of a city's population. Second are a set of urban attributes, elements that help to define the city. Finally, we will examine a set of eight factors that can be described as the city's urban amenities. These three elements will serve to differentiate a city from all others, as well as positioning that city in an array of all of the others.

Chapter 5 – demographics and quality of life

Urban demographics is a set of characteristics of a city that have become front page items in our newspapers. This is certainly true of migration, and racial mix and tension. The Trump administration has turned migration into an issue that divides the population into what has increasingly been described as tribes. But beyond this, migration has been a very positive element in a city's labor force. On the one hand, during the pandemic our television screens have been filled with images of physicians and nurses, as well as researchers, scientists, cleaners, cooks, and medical assistants, among others, and a very significant percentage of them are recent immigrants from countries all over the world. On the other hand, the same is true of the high tech world and its entrepreneurs, researchers, and skilled workers. The Seattles, Austins, Silicon Valleys, and other centers of the US tech world are disproportionately populated with immigrants. Without them we would be a much less advanced place. Any city should seek to maximize this component of its population.

The second element is racial mix and racial tension. The "Black Lives Matter" movement is a monument to the failure of many of our cities to create a climate of tolerance and of diversity. Racial tension served to limit the economic competitiveness of the US South, a deterrent to growth that began to diminish only when the financial and technology sectors attracted a skilled labor force from more tolerant regions of the country. Richard Florida and Melanie Faasche calculate a Global Index of Tolerance every year. (Florida and Fassche) They argue that any city that wants to serve as a host to innovative, talented, and creative people and the firms that employ them simply must be a city with a culture of tolerance with regard to race, gender, sexual identification, religion, national origin, and so forth.

Much has been made recently of the relative growth rate of a city by its population size, the part of the country in which it is situated, and whether the city is an urban center or a suburb. Population growth or decline is an obvious indicator of a healthy or a troubled city. But the issue is not as simple or as causal as it would appear to be at first glance.

Finally, is there an optimal age distribution for a city that seeks a high quality of life? Does a high proportion of seniors mean that the city's cultural institutions will be well supported? Or are there some negative consequences, perhaps on the housing market, or the healthcare sector? One recent study demonstrated that a population of seniors had a set of several positive impacts on a city's economy and that on balance this was a positive element in the urban population. (Kresl and Ietri, esp. p. 174)

Chapter 6 – urban attributes and quality of life

One of the most salient aspects of a high quality of life of any city is the pride its residents take in its history and the development of its most prominent aspects. Some of these accomplishments include, for example, Pittsburgh's history with the steel industry, or St. Louis's rather short-lived identification as the "Gateway to the West", or Rochester's identification with Eastman-Kodak. Residents take pride in this element of their history and it makes them feel good about their city. This pride can become a factor that supports optimism about the future of the city. It serves as a base for identification with the city and a willingness to remain there. Those who study this issue use terms such as "strategic image marketing", and "place promotion" or "place boosterism", to link pride in place to place branding and marketing. (Kavaratzis and Ashworth, ch. 1)

An issue that has received some attention in recent years is that of an optimal size for a city – is there one? Can small cities thrive in a niche in which they are well suited? Are there issues of coordination, transportation, governance, and social cohesion that hinder the ability of a "too large" city to compete effectively? Furthermore, can a city's population density, or the lack of it, be a factor that will act positively or negatively on a city's quality of life?

Another factor that can have an impact on city quality of life is that of isolation or connectedness. This is an issue that is very much "in the eyes of the beholder". Cities of all sizes are linked to large cities, such as New York or Los Angeles. Do their residents sort themselves out in accordance with their preference for close proximity, or connectedness, or sufficient distance to manage their own lives? Is life in rural Montana one of isolation, even if one telecommutes with a firm in Seattle? This is obviously a complex issue.

The final urban attribute we will examine is that of effectiveness of government. The lack of this attribute can be extremely frustrating to one who wants the basic services of government to be reliably provided. One's quality of life can be greatly diminished if one is routinely frustrated in provision of these services.

Chapter 7 – urban amenities and quality of life

There are eight urban amenities we will examine in relation to their impact on quality of life. They are rather straightforward and we will not have to discuss them in detail here. They are essentially the core elements that can be seen as determinants of a city's ability to attract the highly skilled workers of the economy of today and in the future. We have noted above that these workers are highly mobile. In contrast to their predecessors they do not graduate from an educational institute and then work in the town or city in which they grew up. Rather, they move to a city that offers them the aspects of life that are attractive to them. Often they have a family, with young children. What they appear to find attractive is a congenial, safe neighborhood, with good public education, recreation, and cultural institutions – if only so their children will be exposed to music, theater, dance, and art. Public safety, social services, municipal transportation, and quality housing are other important factors. Suitable housing is, of course, at the top of the list.

All of these factors work together to create the quality of life that will make a specific city a place that is attractive to them. Without these amenities, it is highly unlikely that any city will be able to successfully compete with other cities that are successful in putting together an attractive package of urban amenities.

Chapter 8 – looking forward

Examination of the "consequences" of quality of life on a range of elements of human life, and then on the "components" of quality of life takes us to a very broad consideration of the major aspects of our individual and community lives. The concept of "quality of life" has itself evolved during the past several decades, apace with changes in the nature of our economy. All of this may at times appear to be a bit messy or disorganized, but this is in the nature of meeting the needs of individuals in a world of flux.

In the concluding chapter, we will, among other things, consider the nature of quality of life in the world after the initial onslaught of the coronavirus. The perhaps long-term restructuring of the major elements in our economic, social and cultural structures and in our individual and collective lives will have to be considered. The way we move through spaces, our access to healthcare, the impact on social institutions and behaviors, the impact on transportation, property markets, the service sector, entertainment from sports to opera, travel, engagement with other people in other places, and so many other things that make up our quality of life will have to be reconsidered before we conclude our discussion.

REFERENCES

Case, Ann and Angus Deaton, *Deaths of Despair and the Future of Capitalism*, Princeton: Princeton University Press, 2020.

Florida, Richard, *The New Urban Crisis*, New York: Basic Books, 2017.

Florida, Richard and Melanie Faasche, *The Rise of the Urban Creative Class in Southeast Asia*, Toronto: Martin Prosperity Institute, 2017.

Glaeser, Edward, *Triumph of the City: How Our Greatest Invention Makes Us Richer, Smarter, Greener, Healthier, and Happier*, New York: The Penguin Press, 2011.

Katz, Bruce and Jennifer Bradley, *The Metropolitan Revolution: How Cities and Metros are Fixing our Broken Politics and Fragile Economy*, Washington: The Brookings Institution, 2013.

Kavaratzis, Mihalis and Gregory Ashworth, "Place branding: where do we stand?", in Gregory Ashworth and Mihalis Kavaratzis, (eds), *Towards Effective Place Brand Management: Branding European Cities and Regions*, Cheltenham, UK and Northampton, MA, USA: Edward Elgar, pp. 1–14, 2010.

Kresl, Peter Karl and Daniele Ietri, *The Aging Population and the Competitiveness of Cities –Benefits to the Urban Economy*, Cheltenham, UK and Northampton, MA, USA: Edward Elgar, 2010.

Kresl Peter Karl and Balwant Singh, "Urban Competitiveness and US Metropolitan Centres", *Urban Studies*, Vol. 49, No. 2, February 2010, pp. 239–54.

McGregor, J. Allister, Laura Camfield and Alison Woodcock, "Needs, Wants and Goals: Wellbeing, Quality of Life and Public Policy", *Applied Research Quality of Life*, Vol. 4, 2009, pp. 135–54.

Naud, Daniel and Rémy Tremblay, "Discours sur la qualité de vie et la compétitivité des villes du savoir", in Diane-Gabrielle Tremblay and Rémy Tremblay, (eds), *La Compétitivité Urbaine à l'ère de la Nouvelle Économie*, Québec: Presses de l'Université du Québec, pp. 57–66, 2006.

O'Sullivan, Feargus, "Paris Mayor: It's Time for a '15-Minute City'", *CityLab*, 18 February 2020, www.bloomberg.com/citylab.

Shapiro, Jesse M., "Smart Cities: Quality of Life, Productivity, and the Growth Effects of Human Capital", *NBER Working Papers Series*, Working Paper 11615, September 2005.

Sustainable Development Solutions Network, *World Happiness Report*, Paris: United Nations, 20 March 2020.

2. Contemporary analysis of quality of life

Historically, economists have not given much thought to the issue of quality of life. From the beginning, with Adam Smith, the focus has been narrowly on the material aspects of wellbeing – see *The Wealth of Nations*. (Smith) Smith writes of "the real wealth, the annual produce of the land and labour of the society", (p. lx) and, more to the point of this book, in comparing two individuals who choose to spend their revenue in two different ways, "the magnificence of the person whose expense had been chiefly in durable commodities, would be continually increasing, ... that of the other, on the contrary, would be no greater at the end of the period than at the beginning". (p. 330) Smith and his successors have been primarily focused on markets and other mechanisms for the allocation of resources so as to maximize material output, and thereby human wellbeing. There is no place in the thinking of Smith for the non-material elements of quality of life we will be exploring here. The focus was on what is material and what can be measured. The simple notion that more is better than less must be applied to the nation as an entity, if at all. Consuming and using more goods means less time is available for unutilized "free time", and, as will be proposed here, it may be true for many individuals that maximization of goods consumption is not the same as maximization of wellbeing.

This is especially true for the nation as an entity when the distribution of what is produced is skewed to a population that excludes many individuals. Much has been written recently about the distribution of income in contemporary economies and about the stagnation of income for the preponderance of the population, to the benefit of the top one percent. (Atkinson; Milanovic; Stiglitz) One can argue that while national income (GDP) has been increasing, the wellbeing of perhaps the majority of the population in many countries has not risen – more goods and services do not mean higher wellbeing if a small percentage of the population is able to appropriate the majority of what is produced. Furthermore, even the wealthy few may not be happier, or feeling better, if they are surrounded by others who have even more. I grew up in Fox River Grove, Illinois, a small middle class town 40 miles northwest of Chicago. It was also five miles from Barrington Hills, a wealthy town with grand country houses filled with senior corporate people. I would on occasion tend bar at their parties. I remember one in the summer at which I was giving a soft drink to a teenage boy. His father approached him and asked what he had been doing, and the boy said that he had been playing with Bobby. His father got very angry and told him in no uncertain terms that he wanted his son to play with Tommy. Clearly this was a man who was able to rent a house in an area filled with CEOs, etc., and he had one year to be accepted in this community. Hence, his son had to play with the son of someone "important" to his father's future. If this did not work, then it was back to Chicago, with no chance to be invited to join the Barrington Hills Country Club. His income could lead to diminished happiness, and to an incessant struggle for "more", if things did not work out. This is an example of the "transformation problem" in which more goods may not be transformed into wellbeing or happiness. The rich person may in this case not be happier or feel better than another who is poorer but is content with his/her lot. (Bruni, pp. 14–15)

Beyond the impacts on individuals and their material standard of living, Joseph Stiglitz tells us that: "Widely unequal societies do not function efficiently and their economies are neither stable nor sustainable in the long term. When one interest group holds too much power, it succeeds in getting policies that benefit itself, rather than policies that would benefit society as a whole." (Stiglitz, p. 83) The classic example of this was the US Supreme Court 2010 decision on Citizens United, that gave corporations and other entities First Amendment (free speech) rights to act as individuals and to give their financial support to political candidates. This resulted in the development of the Super PACs that have enabled wealthy individuals and corporations they control to greatly enhance the political power of the right-wing of the political spectrum and to introduce policies that work to their material benefit. The distribution of income was not much of an issue until the 1980s when President Reagan lowered personal income taxes at the top end. Before this, when personal income taxes were as high as the 90 percentile range, as they were throughout the 1970s, it was not worth the effort for an executive to lobby for higher income when so much went to the government in taxes. By the late 1990s the rate had fallen to around 30 percent ... the game was on, so to speak.

Thomas Piketty has given us an important analysis of this phenomenon and this period in our history, the past 30 years or so. (Piketty, p. 25) He shows that income inequality in the US and Western Europe was not an issue during the Post-World War II years, until the 1980s. At this point inequality rose to its World War I level in Europe and to that of 1940 in the US. In his analysis the crucial determinant of this rise in inequality was the growth in the importance of the return to capital in relation to the growth in the economy – annual increase in income or output. Whereas the former includes rents, dividends, interest and profit, the latter is production of goods and services and generates wages. Growth in political power of capital owners has been greater than the weakened power of labor unions, hence the rise in income inequality.

The plight of working people has been exacerbated by the course of development of the economy during the past 150 years. Robert Gordon has examined the course of technological development during this period and its impact on both output and the nature of production. (Gordon) During the 1870–1940 period technological advance brought us transformation in the character of our economy. Developments were of a kind that greatly enhanced the mode of living of the entire population – the automobile, electricity for appliances and mechanical devices, the airplane, electric lighting, running water and sewerage, flush toilets, central heating, refrigerators, the telephone – in short there was a dramatic transformation in the way in which the wealthy and working people lived their lives.

Technological change since World War II has been far less than transformative. It has taken about the same time to fly from New York to Los Angeles over the past several decades, when one includes the time spent in the terminal at each end of the voyage (20 minutes as opposed to three hours), the speed of the 737 versus that of the 707, and so forth. Cell phones are convenient but less transformative than the telephone, and, while computers have been transformative per se, the deterioration of the distribution of income has meant, primarily, that for the vast majority of the population this has meant some convenience in entertainment, communications, and retail, but nothing transformative. Working class people have stood on the sidelines and watched while the wealthy population greatly enhance their material disposable income. This has been compellingly portrayed by Matthew Desmond in his powerful book *Evicted.* (Desmond) Low income neighborhoods and towns usually lack access to high-speed internet, or even to internet; without internet it is not possible to participate in whatever advances to wellbeing these post-World War II technological advances have brought. Elevators that soar 45 floors in just a few seconds are of little benefit to someone who lives in a walk-up apartment in a two or three story building.

In these introductory pages of this chapter we have demonstrated that when we limit ourselves to material consumption, the benefits of economic growth will not be widely shared among all sectors of the population. We certainly cannot say that the majority of the population have not been better off materially because of this growth. But this says nothing about the more interesting concept, the quality of life. The notion of quality of life has its own difficulties in definition. It is certainly more than just material output or income. Nonetheless, there has been much research done on this concept, both in its definition and in its measurement.

APPROACHES TO THE QUALITY OF LIFE

The interest of Smith, and his classical economist followers, was in the nation or the individual rather than in the city. However, our interest in this book is in analysis of quality of life at the level of the city. We seek to study the impact of quality of life on an urban economy, its competitiveness, its cohesion, its relationship to firms in the private sector, and to categories of the labor force. However, there are also important things we can learn from examining quality of life at the level of the nation. We will begin with the analysis with regard to the nation and then continue to our principal concern – the city.

At the Level of the Nation

One of the quality of life related initiatives that has become very popular is the notion of an index of happiness. Inspired by the initiative of the government of Bhutan undertaken upon the declaration of the King, in 1972, that the goal of government policy should be focused on Gross National Happiness rather than the traditional Gross National Product, this project to give priority to happiness rather than to the output of material goods and the measurement of happiness has been taken up by the United Nations. (Helliwell, Layard and Sachs, p. 7) The first issue of the World Happiness Report was issued in 2012. At the outset, in the report it was noted that there were many aspects of the lives of the world's inhabitants that were strongly negative in their impacts. Many people lacked enough food, the environment was being destroyed and many were suffering or dying from Case and Deaton's deaths of despair – substance abuse, suicide, obesity, and so forth. The policy response of some has always been to manage a more rapid growth of Gross National Product, but in the report Jeffry Sachs notes that: "GNP is a valuable goal, but should not be pursued to the point where economic stability is jeopardized, community cohesion is destroyed, the vulnerable are not supported, ethical standards are sacrificed, or the world's climate is put at risk ... happiness varies more with quality of human relationships than (with) income". (Sachs, p. 9)

Later in the report, Richard Layard, Andrew Clark and Claudia Senik present a model for happiness that includes both "external" and "personal" determinants. (Layard, Clark and Senik, p. 59) "External" factors as key determinants include income, work, community and governance, and values and religion, and "personal" factors as key determinants include mental health, physical health, family experience, education, and gender and age. In concluding their report, Layard, Clark and Sachs argue (p. 95) that: "As knowledge increases, societies will have a growing basis for a new type of policy-making aimed at increasing happiness and reducing misery. This would involve a change of perspective and a change in the techniques of policy analysis".

By 2019 this approach had been modified to include seven key factors in the construction of the Happiness Index: GDP per capita, social support, healthy life expectancy, generosity, perceptions of corruption, unexplained happiness. (Hugo) This is the index that is reported in the press each year when the new report is issued, and is headed by the Nordic countries, Switzerland, Netherlands, Canada, and New Zealand.

The World Happiness Report gets its data from the Gallup World Poll which asks questions of about 1,000 residents of each of 157 countries. (Hugo) The residents are all over 15 years of age and are randomly selected from individuals who are registered in each country. This gives the result of measured happiness for all countries, with the Nordic countries, Switzerland, Netherlands, Canada, New Zealand, and Australia as the ten happiest countries. At the bottom are countries in southern Africa, the Middle East, and Haiti. Application and analysis of the ranking of 157 countries is left to the reader or analyst.

There is much we can learn from this ranking. Most importantly, growth of GDP and income do not overwhelm the rankings, but are put in a basket of several other variables that are much "softer" such as generosity, social support, health, family relations, values and religion, and gender and age. Thus, monetary and fiscal policy alone cannot make for a "happy" population. This is in line with the "Easterlin paradox", that as a society becomes richer it does not become happier; indeed "the growth process itself engenders ever-growing wants that lead it ever onward" (Easterlin, p. 121), rather like a hungry mule that walks toward some hay that is kept two feet in front of its face. In their study of quality of life in Thailand, J. A. McGregor, L. Camfield and A. Woodcock found that "in the most affluent of countries there are those who repeatedly fail to achieve any meaningful degree of wellbeing, and even in the poorest countries of the South some people achieve surprisingly high levels of wellbeing". (McGregor, Camfield and Woodcock, p. 150)

A second observation which develops this unhappy population notion further is that as young people currently spend more time with cell phones and social media to maintain contact with each other, they paradoxically become more isolated. (Twenge, pp. 89–92) They spend less time interacting with each other face-to-face, going to parties, and in other forms of social interaction. More screen time, with video games and computers, also means less time participating in religious activities, reading books, and even sleeping. All of these activities are components in happiness research findings. Use of digital media has increased significantly among young people in the US since the 1980s. They can be seen as another form of the addiction highlighted by Case and Deaton, above.

At the Level of the City

The UN Happiness Index is developed by having data gathered on the level of the nation, and results or rankings are then given for 157 nations. Unfortunately, by itself this tells us little if anything about quality of life for cities in general, or for any specific city. In order to gain an understanding of quality of life at the level of the city, we will begin with a rather broad brush and then narrow to scope more tightly on "the city" per se.

The spatial arrangement of production, housing, retail, transportation, services and other aspects of the economy during the past two centuries has evolved as incomes, city functions, and populations have developed. In the 19th century, production was situated in proximity to either transportation or a source of power, or it was clustered with other facilities with which the company had production relationships. Workers tended to live within walking distance of the factory, and downtown retail entities tended to cater to the "carriage trade" of wealthier families – for example, Marshall Field's in Chicago (Miller, ch. 9), Wanamaker's in Philadelphia, Dayton's in Minneapolis, Hudson's in Detroit, or Kaufman's in Pittsburgh. Under the influence of the transformative technologies highlighted by Gordon, these linkages began to weaken. As workers' income edged up they became a more attractive clientele for retailers. As cities developed streetcar and bus lines workers sought residential areas that were more congenial and healthy than proximity to a smoky and polluting factory, and the factory-residence tie was broken. Beginning in the 1950s, highway systems using the city center as the hub of a network facilitated movement of residential areas into the suburbs. Ultimately the structure known as "sprawl" came to dominate most large cities.

In recent years a reaction against this has developed. In part it is due to the enormous amount of time that is wasted in commuting, to the demands for gasoline and other energy sources, and to the environmental consequences of so much automobile travel. Suburbs were also often zoned for single family housing only, as a technique for keeping the suburbs white and of an acceptable income level. In Paris, Carlos Moreno, a professor and advisor to the mayor Ann Hidalgo, has proposed the concept of the "intelligent city", or the "city of the quarter of an hour". (Belaich) His idea is that Paris should seek to wean itself away from the time-consuming, polluting and dangerous automobiles and to work toward what Mayor Hidalgo refers to as the "15-minute city". At the center of this notion is Moreno's "six things that make an urbanite happy". This is his notion of happiness, or elements of quality of life, for an urban dweller. They are: "dwelling in dignity, working in proper conditions, (being able to gain) provisions, wellbeing, education and leisure", with wellbeing being a catch-all term for being happy, healthy, and contented. To achieve this, there must be a "thoroughly integrated urban fabric, where stores mix with homes, bars mix with health centers, and schools with office buildings", so as to reduce the perimeter within which these activities are situated. (O'Sullivan)

This notion of reducing the need for mobility is not new in Paris. The 20-minute city was introduced by Portland, Oregon, over ten years ago. It is telling that the initiative was introduced by the city's Office of Sustainable Development and that its primary objective was that of reducing greenhouse-gas emissions. To this end, the city was to promote light-rail transit, commuting by bicycle, and walkable neighborhoods. The resident was to be able "to walk to essential amenities and services in 20 minutes", but not to work – this will remain distinct from the neighborhoods. (Streuteville) Interestingly, an argument given for this is that a walkable city will result in people being healthier and that this will reduce insurance premiums. Since there are no major insurance companies in Portland, this should save Portlanders about $800 million (2005 dollars). (Camner) There is no speculation as to what Portlanders would do with this financial windfall, but this is rather far from the six objectives of Carlos Moreno and Mayor Hidalgo in Paris.

With regard to Paris, close proximity to cultural institutions and public performance spaces are, naturally, also stressed. Additionally, the initiative of Paris comes after several years of pursuing Portland's objectives – reducing access to the city by the most polluting cars, banning vehicles from the streets next to the Seine, and converting some road ways for pedestrians and trees and other greenery. While many other cities have been attracted to the approach of Portland to reducing greenhouse gasses and automobile usage, the approach of Paris which is closer to the issue of this book, quality of life, has been less attractive to them. In the US this is to a large extent due to the fact that our cities are neither burdened nor blessed with physical layouts that date back hundreds of years. With the exception of a few city centers such as those of Savannah, Santa Fe and Philadelphia, and lower Manhattan, most of our cities lack the dense proximity of residence, work, culture and retail of Paris.

One of the first issues we must treat is that of the benefit of studying quality of life at all. During the 1980s there was considerable emphasis given to the notion that all that mattered in competitiveness was attracting capital to a city. This is, of course, based on the conceptualization of the economy during the manufacturing era into the 1980s and 1990s. Stephen Walters puts this clearly: "one key attraction of cities, for both the virtuous and venal, is their abundant, durable, and immobile capital ... We may tend to think of cities as dense concentrations of people, but we need to start thinking of them as accumulations of capital in all its forms that help residents to flourish materially, socially and culturally." (Walters, p. 10) The impetus during the latter decades of the 20th century into the current century to do whatever was needed to attract capital to a city resulted in the notion of quality of life being "constructed to meet the demands of capital". It is generally argued that tending to the needs of capital will gradually extend to the rest of the (laboring) population. However, Rogerson finds that "little emphasis has been given to those studies which consider that quality of life is concerned with life satisfaction and happiness", rather than to the needs of accommodating capital, and that "other people feel marginalized". (Rogerson, pp. 980)

A sharp contrast to the notion that quality of life is tied to the needs of capital attraction is that which comes from the study of health and of ageing. While this approach is as inwardly focused as is that on capital, it does have the advantage of placing humans at the center of its analysis. Ann Bowling has done an early study of this aspect of quality of life and, in a survey she administered, demonstrated that the most important items were: relations with family, one's own health and that of someone close, and finances/housing/ standard of living. Barely mentioned were items related to work, social life, leisure, education, and religion. (Bowling, p. 1451) One aspect of quality of life studies is that they rarely can be quantified, but rather rely on individual respondents giving their qualitative evaluation of the importance of individual elements in the survey. Nonetheless one can differentiate respondents by sex, marital status, age, education and so forth. In Bowling's study, she reports that while males list ability to do work and social life more highly than do females, the latter are more likely to identify depression and anxiety as significant. Younger respondents were more responsive with regard to ability to do work, and to have a social life and a sex life. Older respondents were more responsive when asked about mobility, gardening, shopping, and simply to be able to stand and walk. (Bowling, p. 1457) Often these studies give results that are not surprising, but they do add some confirmation to our expectations and are useful in justifying certain social or economic policies as components of a personalized notion of quality of life.

An early study of quality of life with a broader focus than that of Bowling was done by Glenn C. Blomquist, Mark C. Berger and John P. Hoehn (B-B-H) in 1988. They focused on wages, rents, and amenities, and ranked 253 urban counties, for 1980. The counties do not capture the ranking for any city of size, as they will be composed of more than one county. The quality of life indices are converted into dollar values and range from $3,388.72, for Pueblo county, Colorado, #1, to –$1856.70 for St. Louis (City), #253. It is interesting to see what they give as results for the counties of a larger city. For example, Denver consists of five counties: Arapahoe (#3 and $2097), Boulder (#12 and $1320), Denver (#14 and $1295), Adams (#53 and $727), and Jefferson (#62 and $609); St. Louis also consists of five counties: St. Clair, Illinois, (#195 and –$251), St. Charles (#221 and –$486), St. Louis (#240 and –$875), Jefferson (#242 and –$918), and St. Louis City (#253 and –$1875). The spread of the rankings of these counties is informative and identifies clearly which counties have a high quality of life and which do not.

The variables used to calculate these rankings are, however, relevant to an earlier economy than the one we have today. The 16 variables consist of seven relating to climate – such as precipitation, sunshine, temperature and humidity, and six relating to environment – visibility, landfill waste, superfund sites and disposal sites. This leaves three variables to capture the richness of amenities (to be discussed in detail in Chapter 6). There is one relating to crime (violent crime), one to education (teacher–pupil ratio), and one to whether the city is or is not a central city. The amenities were expected to be incorporated into differences in wages and rents, and it is these variables that would generate inducements for workers to select their place of residence and of work. The highest ranked locations were smaller and medium-sized cities in the Sun Belt and Colorado. New York, Chicago, Philadelphia and other northern, and older, cities tended to be clustered at the bottom of the rankings. Similar results were given in Mark Berger, Glenn Blomquist and Werner Waldner. (Blomquist, Berger and Hoehn, p. 105; and Berger, Blomquist and Waldner, p. 777)

James Burnell and George Galster examined this approach, which they referred to as the "market/resident approach" since housing and wages are thought to compensate for quality-of-life differences. They compare its results with those of what they refer to as the "livability comparisons approach" of the *Places Rated Almanac* which compares urban regions through use of a set of objective indicators that relate to quality of life. (Boyer and Savageau) Their primary interest is whether there is a pattern between the values of a quality-of-life index and urban population size. Burnell and Galster converted the quality-of-life values to Z-scores, so they were compatible, and regressed the scores on the population of a large set of SMSA populations (using data for 1980). Both are strongly related; however the results are dramatically different. (Burnell and Galster, pp. 728–9) For Boyer and Savageau the values are directly related to city size, and the maximum value occurs at a population of 4.4 million. The Berger, Blomquist and Waldner results are quite the opposite, in that the relationship between city size and quality of life are negative and optimal city size would be, as noted above, a population of a few hundred thousand residents.

The authors add that the conclusion of the ranking is the notion that amenities are important elements in economic wellbeing. However the amenities included in this project would not be very likely to induce much movement of workers today. To begin with, there is no objective way to give the climate of a particular city or region a rating that would be accepted by most individuals. Does one like to ski or play golf? I have lived in Austin but I would vastly prefer to live in Montreal, etc. Violent crime, or the lack thereof, and the teacher–pupil ratio don't capture the qualities of specific neighborhoods sufficiently to serve as inducements to relocation, at least not for today's labor force. Furthermore, what is it that is moving in response to these amenities?

Some of the research is done with the intention of ascertaining what quality of life elements will induce companies to relocate, rather than workers: "it is unsurprising that capital and the state find quality of life ratings so useful". (Rogerson, p. 983) Lorna Wallace wrote, in 1999, that "Quality of life considerations can be important attributes of a site but the importance varies according to the size of the locating company: individual preferences of its top management; and the activity to be undertaken". The decision to locate is up to "individual preferences of management, their perceived preferences of employees, and upon economic and other operating costs". (Wallace, p. 21) Employees participate only to the degree that management understands what their preferences are. This is clearly backward looking rather than anticipating the world of mobile and in demand workers that is to come.

More in line with today's economy are Gülnur Çevikayak and Koray Velibeyoglu writing about technology districts and stating that there are three elements involved – business requirements, spatial requirements and requirements of "knowledge workers". With regard to the latter they state that: "Locating in a vibrant environment is important because of the need to supply talented, highly skilled workers with desirable quality of life in an integrated living, working and playing area". (Çevikayak and Velibeyoglu, p. 43) They look to drawing highly skilled workers to a location rather than assuming that just because there is a company located in a place they will be drawn to it. Richard Florida put it very succinctly: "Companies were the force behind the old game and cities measured their status by the number of corporate headquarters they were home to …. But while companies remain important, they no longer call all the shots … Companies increasingly go, and are started, where talented and creative people are". (Florida, p. 283)

An important approach to amenities and quality of life was offered by Mark Partridge when he reviewed three approaches to regional growth: the New Economic Geography (NEG) model, for which Paul Krugman is the primary figure, the agglomeration economies approach of Michael Storper and Allen Scott, and the natural amenity migration approach of Philip Graves. (Krugman, Storper and Scott and Graves) Partridge wrote in 2010, with data being 2008 at the latest. (Partridge) He finds that the NEG model missed the substantial movement of population from the Core (Chicago–Philadelphia–Boston). The essence of the NEG model is pecuniary externalities, and agglomeration economies, with transportation costs also being a significant factor. This would not have predicted the significant movement of people from the Core to the Sunbelt and the West. Following World War II the South suffered outmigration (including the Great Migration of African Americans) from its agriculture to the automobile, steel and other manufacturing cities of the Core, and it was not until the 1980s that this was reversed. Thus NEG looked backward and missed the big events of the end of the 20th century.

The South lost population until the impacts of rural electrification, TVA water projects, the automobile, the telephone, rail transportation from Chicago and New York to, among other places, New Orleans, Atlanta, and Miami, and finally air travel were fully realized in the 1960s and later years. This led to the North to South migration that has extended powerfully into the 21st century. Partridge argues that Storper and Scott err in rejecting the notion of amenity-led growth. He notes that: "given that the South and Rocky Mountain regions – two areas blessed with natural amenities – faced significant economic barriers in the mid-20th century, it would be very hard to expect that given their initial economic and institutional conditions (and their pre-1960 track record), they would be strong candidates for endogenous growth" – but this is just what happened. (Partridge, p. 9)

In the 21st century with much of the labor force possessing enhanced technical ability, knowledge, and mobility, and when many of them are younger than earlier work forces, less place-connected and more into recreation, beaches and other social life natural amenities have become more powerful inducements to mobility. Amenity migration may be responsive to amenities other than natural ones, so the future movements of workers are hard to forecast. But it is clear that with developments in technology, less exclusionary national borders, and standardization of important things such as healthcare, we should expect there to be enhanced migration, albeit to a new set of amenities, not just the natural ones. Both Partridge and Graves thus give authenticity to the notion that amenities are important elements in the study of quality of life.

This is supported by Jess Shapiro in a study of the determinants of city employment growth. He notes that many studies note the correlation between human capital and local employment, but finds the causation to be unexplained. (Shapiro, p. 2) He finds there are three possible explanations for this. First, some variable could have been omitted by researchers. Second, highly educated populations generate higher productivity growth. Third, more educated populations experience a higher growth in quality of life. The latter could be either because more educated people generate a higher growth of consumption amenities where they live, or because they have greater influence on the political process, leading to lower crime and pollution.

To address the first possibility he added two variables for aspects of education, at the university level (presence of land-grant institutions) and compulsory schooling laws. This adjustment had no significant impact. For the remaining two possibilities he used a neoclassical growth model to ascertain what share in employment growth of human capital was due to productivity growth and what was due to improvements in the quality of life. His conclusion is that about 60 percent of the effect of college graduates on growth of employment is due to productivity growth, but that the remainder "comes from the relationship between concentrations of skill and growth in the quality of life". (Shapiro, p. 3) When he examines the relationship between human capital and measures of quality of life, he finds "the effect may be operating through the expansion of consumer amenities such as bars and restaurants rather than through the political process". The political process would have had its impact through improvements to crime, schools and pollution, but the consumer amenities mechanism is far more powerful in its impact.

A similar result is achieved by Michael Luger who examines quality of life impacts on the "sorting out" of businesses and individuals in their locational decisions. He concurs with Shapiro that until very recently the focus in studies on inter-metro movements was on taxes, infrastructure and public services, and the company movement was the issue; however, by the early 1990s the focus had shifted on the movements of individuals/workers. (Luger, p. 749) For him, the crucial quality of life elements now include public safety, recreational and cultural opportunities, housing, healthcare "and similar amenities that can be affected by public and private sector actions, as well as climate and other natural characteristics of a geographic area". He does note some difficulty with the related variables, such as that high education expenses can be an indication of a well-educated community where people value education, or of a low-income one in which education spending is being used to bring the community into a better and preferred situation. I would offer that one cannot simply assume that people will prefer to have lower taxes. A couple of decades ago the electorate in Sweden voted out of office a Conservative government because one of the campaign items was lower taxes! Swedes wondered what will happen to healthcare, roads, educational institutions, etc. if taxes were reduced. Bring on Labor!

It is also necessary not to just look at tax rates, when studying quality of life and locational issues, it is also necessary, noted Paul Gottlieb, to take into account the value of the services that are purchased with those taxes. He states that: "the existence of high-technology firms in costly, high-amenity regions is perfectly compatible with careful economic models of *profit* maximization". (Gottlieb, p. 280) His conclusion is that those who are interested in economic development, in the modern economy, must take into account the provision of residential amenities, and quality of living considerations, and ignore these elements "at their peril".

A good example of this is given by Eugene McCann in a study of the "best places" rankings, such as that of *Money* magazine, in the thinking of city development managers and committees. A feature of the *Money* rankings is that they are compiled through questionnaires submitted by 500 of its subscribers, who are asked to rank 40 city characteristics on a scale of 1 to 10 with regard to the place being a good place to live. The median income of the group was $78,000 (in the mid-1990s) and the median age was 48. Respondents sought a city with low property and personal crime, and an appreciating housing market. Rochester, Minnesota, was highly ranked, presumably because the 48-year olds were concerned with high quality healthcare and the Mayo Clinic is located in Rochester. (McCann, p. 1914) It is not clear what this all says about either quality of life or an economically competitive city. Nonetheless, McCann finds that economic planners in many cities are very familiar with, and devoted to, the *Money* rankings, and notes that the magazine "explicitly defines its 'best places' in terms of their quality of life, including not only their potential for new investors but also their 'extra-economic', social and cultural, characteristics". (McCann, p. 1918)

The example McCann discusses at some length is the experience of Austin, Texas, consistently ranked as one of the top ten cities, noting that the city "has achieved both high levels of livability and economic growth, making it a model combination of an ideal home town and an economic boomtown". And he quotes the magazine as noting that: "Austin wouldn't make MONEYs Best Places list if it were just a tech boomtown ... (It also) boasts symphonies, art museums, film festivals, good restaurants and good football as well as some of the best live music in the country". (McCann, pp. 1919–20) He sees Austin's economic development managers as having a conceptualization of quality of life as being at the center of the city's success as a place to be studied and emulated. He closes by noting that an important question for all who celebrate a city's quality of life is – "a good place for whom?". Those who know Austin (as well as any other US city) will think of the East Side with its concentration of lower income Hispanics and African Americans, who may not be participating in the city's celebrated quality of life.

It should be clear by now that it is difficult to agree upon a single approach even to the meaning of the term "quality of life". Ed Diener and Eunkook Suh address this by noting that there are three distinct approaches to defining and measuring the term. The first is based on a set of social indicators – health and medical facilities available, public security and crime, for example. The second consists of measures of the perception or feeling of subjective well-being as expressed by individuals. The third is economic indices that include items such income, prices and unemployment. While the latter tend to be the most utilized when reviewing quality of life, Diener and Suh show that each approach contains vital information not covered by the others. One value of the first two approaches is that they can be referred to when there are questions as to whether more income or greater economic growth are, in fact, desirable. As we have seen, greater economic growth can lead to income inequality and to actual impoverishment of some sectors of the population, whether they are defined simply by income or by race, color and other descriptive classifications. Changes in economic indicators, such as unemployment, have impacts on social indicators, such as health and public security, and, of course, on subjective aspects such as satisfaction with life and relations with friends and family. So the three must be treated in unison for an accurate understanding of quality of life. "Instead of turf battles over who has the best indicator, each discipline needs to borrow insights about quality of life from the other fields." (Diener and Suh, p. 213)

An interesting, albeit somewhat tangential, approach to quality of life in a town or city is offered by Deborah and James Fallows in their book, *Our Towns*. (Fallows and Fallows, pp. 402–408) They list several of the usual elements for quality of life – residents are engaged in the story of their town, and in its development, they have viable downtowns, are near a research university and have a community college or a university, they have distinctive schools, they are tolerant and they have plans for the future. Then they identify another feature that identifies a town with high quality of life – the town has a craft brewery! This is a rapidly expanding industry and they argue that having one is "one of the most reliable signs of civic energy", and indicates the town has a "certain kind of entrepreneurship, and a critical mass of young consumers". The Fallows' approach is unique but it does capture an aspect of quality of life!

One of the first to write about the "creative city" and its quality of life was Charles Landry, *The Creative City*, in 2000. He writes of the need to embed a "culture of creativity" in a city or town. This involves: (1) urban policy that encourages creativity and innovation, (2) developing a creative milieu, (3) building links between technological, economic, social and environmental factors and cultural creativity and innovation, (4) long-term time scales, and (5) attracting to the city the new skills that are self-sustaining. (Landry, p. 79) In order to achieve this, it is necessary to celebrate diversity, maintain distinctiveness and harness creativity. To this end it is necessary to develop: (1) local cultural identity and pride, (2) imagination and creativity, (3) diversity of lifestyle, livelihood, culture and habitat, (4) local distinctiveness, (5) a dynamic local culture, and (6) investment, empowerment and education. Much of this would be included in an understanding of quality of life.

Six years later, Landry addressed quality of life directly, in *The Art of City-Making*. In a list of inward investment factors there are "hard" factors and "soft" factors. Most of the "soft factors" are subsumed under the heading "quality of life". Of 11 hard and soft factors, the one that was mentioned most consistently by respondents in a survey was quality of life – by 25 out of 30 respondents. (Wong) Writing with Phil Wood, he concluded that "soft" factors, such as quality of life or culture, are increasing in significance and that when the decision to enter the city is down to a couple of factors, "'soft' considerations become a 'must-have' factor for locations aiming to attract and retain highly skilled personnel (when quality of life/quality of place is an issue)". (Landry and Wood, p. 285)

Within Landry's creative city, Richard Florida explored the creative class and in the course of examining this gives clarity to the factors that will attract and retain this element of the workforce. He asks the question: "How do you build a truly Creative Community?", and his response is that cities have to create a people climate more than they do a business climate. (Florida, 2002, ch. 16) The crucial factor is clearly the talented and highly mobile younger members of the creative class. In his next book he got more specific, arguing that there were "3Ts" of development in the creative class economy. (Florida, 2012, chs. 12 and 15) First, is Technology. In an earlier era the important technologies had to do with metallurgy, electronic machinery, transportation, and so forth. Today it is "software, robotics and biotechnology". Second, is Talent. Skilled, ambitious, entrepreneurial, educated and ambitious. The linkage between these first two "Ts" has become explicit and dominant today. Third, is Tolerance. The contribution of immigrants is accepted everywhere except in the White House of today. Full acceptance of all sexual preferences, all religions, all races – this is what comprises Tolerance, and it is becoming a *sine qua non* for a creative city. Landry reminds us that "Historically the great cities of the world, have been hubs of ethnicity where the interplay helped achieve their prosperity, innovativeness and stature, although people often lived parallel lives". (Landry, 2006, p. 254)

The university is an institution in which all three of the "Ts" are powerfully present. They are the key centers of both technology and talent, populated as they are with scholars, researchers, and consultants in all areas of the relevant tech economy. They are also one of the first places of refuge sought by individuals who do not conform to the generally accepted models of appearance, behavior and belief. Clearly, they are seeking a high and specific quality of life that can only be found in special places. The "3Ts" have two important elements: they attract a special and crucial element of the labor force, and they work to retain it as well. Many of the studies of quality of life we have examined include the presence of a university or college as a positive element. Robert Lang contrasts major university cities such as Austin and Madison, major creative class centers, with large metropolitan centers that lack a major university such as Las Vegas and Phoenix. Although, when he wrote in 2005, the president of Arizona State University was explicitly attempting to develop the university as a stimulant to Phoenix's Creative Class. (Lang, p. 323) A cautionary note is offered by a team of European researchers who find that for cities in Europe two of Florida's notions do not hold. First, workers in Europe are not as mobile and responsive to attractive amenities as they are in North America. This applies both to international and intranational movement. It is generally accepted that Europeans tend to be more rooted in place than their North American counterparts. Second, in Europe the soft factors (amenities, Florida's 3Ts) are important when a person chooses a district of a city in which to live, but of little importance when choosing the city itself. (Martin-Brelot, Grossetti, Eckert, Gritsai and Kovács, pp. 867–8)

Lang also faults Florida on the lack of sociological theory that underlies his work, basing his own approach in the sociology of Louis Wirth and Herbert Gans, among others. In particular he refers us to the work of Claude Fischer, who developed a model that gives a more solid underpinning of the notion of the creative class, and to how and where it develops. He offers a set of four propositions that explain the influence of urbanism. The more urban a place: (1) the greater its subcultural variety, (2) the more intense its subcultures, (3) the more numerous the sources of diffusion and the greater the diffusion into a subculture, and (4) the higher the rates of unconventionality. He also offers the proposition that: "Cultural differences between urban and rural persons are persistent." As a final comment he offers: "The theory presented here explains the 'evil' and the 'good' of cities simultaneously. Criminal unconventionality and innovative (e.g., artistic) unconventionality are both nourished by vibrant subcultures". (Fischer, pp. 1324–37) One of these subcultures is Florida's creative class.

WHAT IS QUALITY OF LIFE?

As is clear from the preceding text, both the definition of quality of life and its importance have changed over the years as the nature of the economy and the related society have evolved. Until the 1990s the focus was on attracting capital and company location. Companies assumed they would be able to find the labor they needed in proximity to their location. Improving some amenities to enhance the quality of life so as to attract the needed workers did not seem to be an issue of importance. Robert Rogerson discussed this need of some of the earlier writers to be accommodating to capital and to focus almost exclusively on capital. Some of the individuals we included in this chapter have discussed elements that are required for urban competitiveness, and some of them are amenities that could be included in a conceptualization of quality of life.

In Table 2.1 below we have all of the elements in the definition of quality of life of the seven studies we have reviewed in this chapter, beginning with the earliest of Bloomquist, Berger and Hoehn/Waldner in 1987 through to the most recent of Moreno in 2019. The date of each study is given below the name(s) of the writer(s). In Bloomquist et al. and in Bowling items above the line are primary and those below are thought to be of lesser importance. None of the other lists are ranked in any order of priority. As we move from 1987 up to 2019 we notice that the character of the lists evolves in line with the evolution in the economy from manufacturing to information technology. In Bloomquist et al. the traditional items are highlighted – wages and rents, and amenities. Items below the line are of lesser importance. As noted in the text above, there are seven variables listed under climate, and six under environment, so that out of 25 determinants, only amenities, one relating to education

Table 2.1   *Definitions of quality of life*

Bloomquist, Berger and Hoehn/ Waldner	Bowling	Luger	Diener and Suh	Landry	Fallows	Moreno
1987 and 1988	1995	1996	1997	2000 and 2003	2018	2019
Wages	Family relations	Public safety	Health facilities	Local pride	Civic engagement	Dwelling in dignity
Rents	Own health	Recreation	Public security	Imagination and creativity	Viable downtown	Working conditions
Amenities	Health of others	Culture	Subjective wellbeing	Lifestyle Diversity	Research university	Access to provisions
Climate	Finances	Housing	Income	Local culture	Good schools	Wellbeing
Environment	Housing	Healthcare	Prices	Local distinctiveness	Tolerance Plans for future brew pub	Education Leisure
Violent crime	*Standard of living*	Public and private sector amenities	Unemployment	Investment and empowerment		
Teacher– pupil ratio	Social life	Climate		Education		
Central city?	Work					
	Leisure					
	Education					
	Religion					

Source: Author's calculations

and one to crime can be linked with quality of life as we think of it today. Bowling is similar, to a degree, in that after listing the three determinants that relate to the primary focus of her study, health, she highlights three traditional variables – finances, housing and standard of living. The five determinants that are more likely to be stressed today are again, as with Bloomquist, et al., under the line and considered to be of lesser importance.

Diener and Suh lie between the traditional focus of Bloomquist, et al., and Bowling with their focus on income, prices and unemployment, and more contemporary thinking as they then add subjective wellbeing, security, and health to their definition. However, the real transition between the traditional and the contemporary approaches is offered by Luger. Housing is his link to the past, but the rest of his items are more contemporary: culture, recreation, public safety, and public and private sector amenities would all be on the list of quality of life items that would be of importance to today's workforce. As I noted above, climate is in the eye of the viewer!

The real breakthrough occurs with Landry as he ignores the traditional focus on narrowly economic factors, wages, housing, and finances, and gives a list of seven items that would be appropriate to the creative society about which he was writing and in which we have at least one foot today. Diversity, creativity, and local culture are absent in the items "above the line" in Bloomquist, et al., and Bowling. Landry is, of course, writing about a "creative city" so we should expect this, but he does, nonetheless, serve as a useful guide to us today when we consider the elements in a definition of quality of life.

The two remaining writers, the Fallows and Moreno have cut all ties with the past and write only of items that are divorced from traditional economic considerations. The Fallows got their impressions and information over a period of two years in which they flew a small airplane all over the US in a journey of 100,000 miles. Their impressions would very naturally be quite different in nature from the conclusions of an academic study, which is what the six other writers offer us. But in their own way they present their understanding of the quality of life in each of the cities and towns they visit, and it is quite fascinating and informative.

Some of the writers in this chapter have had one eye on urban competitiveness and view amenities and quality of life as elements in this aspect of the life of a city. Some have seen the corporation as the central element as it seeks to maximize its benefit from locating its facility or facilities in specific sites according its own locational criteria. As we approach the contemporary environment the focus is less on the corporation and more on the aspects of the city itself. Economic factors gradually give way to factors that speak to the environment and character of the city itself. Finally, the last and most contemporary of the writers on quality of life, Moreno, works with a new conceptualization of the city and of how it relates to the people who live in it. Moreno writes of "six things that make an urbanite happy", and in order to make the urbanite happy, that is to have a high quality of life, we must reconsider how the people relate to the city and to its space. His six elements work within an urban space that is re-sized for a period of time in which all, or almost all, of the things an urbanite needs should be within a 15-minute bike ride or walk. This reduces the need for automobiles and other vehicles, however they are powered – gas or electric, creates human scale urban spaces, invigorates neighborhoods and increases friendliness and collegiality among the residents of the "neighborhood". Clearly this presents us with a new and distinctive notion of quality of life, in an urban setting.

Before leaving analysis of quality of life, we should note that this is not a measuring stick against which all cities must be measured. That is, there is no single notion of quality of life. We have stressed in this chapter, and will stress elsewhere in this book, a particular notion of quality of life that is most appropriate to the economic issues that confront us today and that will confront us in the foreseeable future. This is an economy that must stress highly skilled, highly mobile, ambitious and, often, family oriented younger workers. The city that will be attractive to them will have to present to them certain elements of quality of life, those that have been identified and stressed in this chapter. But all cities have a quality of life, one that is composed of that city's specific characteristics, and elements that will not be very attractive to the targeted workforce. A city, such as Youngstown or Lewisburg (Pennsylvania) where I live, has a distinctive quality of life that is composed of its own set of characteristics, characteristics that we or the targeted workforce may or may not find to be very attractive. However, it may have larger and cheaper houses, access to outdoor activities such as hunting and fishing, a strong specific ethnic community with its music, festivals, bars, and food, a slower pace of life, and access to a scenic, rural, landscape. At the same time this smaller, less top-20 city, may have good access to the cultural assets of one or more large cities as well as to a major international airport. Kresl did a study of many of these smaller towns and cities and found many of them to be very high in a specific conception of quality of life, but certainly not that of New York or Chicago. (Kresl, 2016) James and Deborah Fallows also found this to be the case in their trip visiting 29 smaller towns. (Fallows) So perhaps one should think of qualities of life, some sub-sets of which comprise the quality of life of a specific city or town, with qualities of life including, among others, amenities, healthcare, public safety, access to transportation, economic assets, and political stability.

REFERENCES

Atkinson, Anthony B., *Inequality: What Can Be Done?*, Cambridge: Harvard University Press, 2015.

Belaich, Charlotte, "Municipales à Paris: Il Faut Déconstruire la Ville Segmentée", *Liberation*, 20 January 2020.

Berger, Mark C., Glenn C. Blomquist and Werner Waldner, "A Revealed-preference Ranking of Quality of Life for Metropolitan Areas", *Social Science Quarterly*, Vol. 68, No. 4, December 1987, pp. 761–78.

Blomquist, Glenn C., Mark Berger and John P. Hoehn, "New Estimates of Quality of Life in Urban Areas", *The American Economic Review*, Vol. 78, No. 1, March 1988, pp. 89–107.

Bowling, Ann, "What Things are Important in People's Lives? A Survey of the Public's Judgements to Inform Scales of Health Related Quality of Life," *Social Science and Medicine*, Vol. 41, No. 10, 1995, pp. 1447–62.

Boyer, R. and D. Savageau, *Places Rated Almanac*, New York: Rand McNally, 1985.

Bruni, Luigno, "Economics, wellbeing and happiness: a historical perspective", in David Maddison, Katrin Rehdanz and Heinz Welsch, (eds), *Handbook on Wellbeing, Happiness and the Environment, Cheltenham, UK and Northampton*, MA, USA: Edward Elgar, 2020.

Burnell, James D. and George Galster, "Quality-of-life Measurements and Urban Size: An Empirical Note", *Urban Studies*, Vol. 29, No. 5, 1992, pp. 727–35.

Camner, Lisa, "The People in Your Neighborhood", *The Atlantic*, 11 May 2010.

Çevikayak, Gülnur and Koray Velibeyoglu, "Organizing: spontaneously developed urban technology precincts", in Tan Yigitcanlar, Kostas Metaxiotis and Francisco Javier Carrillo (eds), *Building Prosperous Knowledge Cities: Policies, Plans and Metrics*, Cheltenham, UK and Northampton, MA, USA: Edward Elgar, 2012.

Desmond, Matthew, *Evicted*, New York: Broadway Books, 2016.

Diener, Ed and Eunkook Suh, "Measuring Quality of Life: Economic, Social, and Subjective Indicators", *Social Indicators Research*, Vol. 40, 1997, pp. 189–216.

Easterlin, Richard, "Does economic growth improve the human lot? Some empirical evidence", in P. A. David and M. W. Reder, (eds), *Nations and Households in Economic Growth: Essays in Honor of Moses Abramovitz*, New York: Academic Press, pp. 89–125, 1974.

Fallows, James and Deborah Fallows, *Our Towns*, New York: Pantheon Books, 2018.

Fischer, Claude S., "Toward a Subcultural Theory of Urbanism", *American Journal of Sociology*, May 1975, pp. 1329–41.

Florida, Richard, *The Rise of the Creative Class*, New York: Basic Books, 2002.

Florida, Richard, *The Rise of the Creative Class, Revisited*, New York: Basic Books, 2012.

Gordon, Robert J., *The Rise and Fall of American Growth, The U.S. Standard of Living Since the Civil War*, Princeton: Princeton University Press, 2016.

Gottlieb, Paul D., "Amenities as an Economic Development Tool: Is there Enough Evidence?," *Economic Development Quarterly*, Vol. 8, No. 3, August 1994, pp. 270–85.

Graves, Philip E., "A Life-Cycle Empirical Analysis of Migration and Climate By Race", *Journal of Urban Economics*, Vol. 6, No. 2, 1979, pp. 135–47.

Helliwell, John, Richard Layard and Jeffrey Sachs, (eds), *World Happiness Report*, New York: The Earth Institute, Columbia University, 2012.

Hugo, "Happiness Index: What is it and How Does it Work", *Tracking Happiness*, 23 May 2019.

Kresl, Peter Karl, *Smaller Cities in a World of Competitiveness*, Abingdon: Routledge, 2016.

Krugman, Paul, "Increasing Returns and Economic Geography", *Journal of Political Economy*, Vol. 99, 1991, pp. 483–99.

Landry, Charles, *The Art of City Making*, London: Earthscan, 2006.

Landry, Charles, *The Creative City, A Toolkit for Urban Innovators*, London: Earthscan, 2000.

Landry, Charles and Phil Wood, *Harnessing and Exploiting the Power of Culture for Competitive Advantage*, Liverpool: Liverpool City Council and the Core Cities Group, 2003.

Lang, Robert E., "The sociology of the creative class", in Diane-Gabrielle Tremblay and Rémy Tremblay, (eds), *La compétitivité urbaine à l'ère de la nouvelle économie*, Québec: Presses de l'Université du Québec, pp. 317–23, 2006.

Layard, Richard, Andrew Clark and Claudia Senik, "The causes of happiness and misery", in John Helliwell, Richard Layard and Jeffrey Sachs, (eds), *World Happiness Report*, New York: The Earth Institute, Columbia University, pp. 58–90, 2012.

Luger, Michael I., "Quality-of-life differences and urban and regional outcomes: a review", *Housing Policy Debate*, Washington: Fannie Mae Foundation, pp. 749–71, 1996.

Martin-Brelot, Helene, Michel Grossetti, Denis Eckert, Olga Gritsai and Zoltán Kovács, "The Spatial Mobility of the 'Creative Class': A European Perspective", *International Journal of Urban and Regional Research*, Vol. 34, No. 4, December 2010, pp. 854–70.

McCann, Eugene J., "'Best Places': Interurban Competition, Quality of Life and Popular Media Discourse", *Urban Studies*, Vol. 41, No. 10, September 2004, pp. 1909–29.

McGregor, J. Allister, Laura Camfield and Alison Woodcock, "Needs, Wants and Goals: Wellbeing, Quality of Life and Public Policy", *Applied Research Quality of Life*, Vol. 4, 2009, pp. 135–54.

Milanovic, Branko, *Global Inequality, A New Approach for the Age of Globalization*, Cambridge: The Belknap Press of Harvard University Press, 2016.

Miller, Donald L., *City of the Century, The Epic of Chicago and the Making of America*, New York: Simon and Schuster, 1996.

O'Sullivan, Feargus, "Paris Mayor: It's Time for a '15-Minute City'", *CityLab*, 18 February 2020, www.bloomberg.com/citylab.

Partridge, Mark D., "The Dueling Models: NEG vs Amenity Migration in Explaining U.S. Engines of Growth", *Papers in Regional Science*, Vol. 89, No. 3, 2010, pp. 513–36.

Piketty, Thomas, *Capital in the Twenty-first Century*, Cambridge: The Belknap Press of Harvard University Press, 2014.

Rogerson, Robert J., "Quality of Life and City Competitiveness", *Urban Studies*, Vol. 36, Nos. 5–6, pp. 969–85, 1999.

Sachs, Jeffrey, "Introduction", in John Helliwell, Richard Layard and Jeffrey Sachs, (eds), *World Happiness Report*, New York: The Earth Institute, Columbia University, pp. 1–9, 2012.

Scott, Allen J., *A World in Emergence, Cities and Regions in the 21st Century*, Cheltenham, UK and Northampton, MA, USA: Edward Elgar, 2012.

Shapiro, Jesse M., *Smart Cities: Quality of Life, Productivity, and the Growth Effects of Human Capital*, Working Paper 11615, Cambridge: National Bureau of Economic Research, September 2005.

Smith, Adam, *An Inquiry into the Nature and Causes of The Wealth of Nations*, New York: Modern Library, 1935.

Stiglitz, Joseph, *The Price of Inequality, How Today's Divided Society Endangers our Future*, New York: W. W. Norton, 2015.

Storper, Michael and Allen J. Scott, "Rethinking Human Capital, Creativity and Human Growth", *Journal of Economic Geography*, Vol, 9, 2009, pp. 147–67.

Streuteville, Robert, "Portland pursues the '20-minute neighborhood'", *Public Square*, 1 September 2008.

Twenge, Jean M., "The sad state of happiness in the United States and the role of digital media", in John Helliwell, Richard Layard and Jeffrey Sachs, (eds), *World Happiness Report*, Paris: Sustainable Development Solutions Network, United Nations, pp. 86–95, 2019.

Wallace, Lorna H., "Foreign direct investment in the USA", in John H. Dunning, (ed.), *Regions, Globalization, and the Knowledge-based Economy*, Oxford: Oxford University Press, 2000.

Walters, Stephen J. K., *Boom Towns, Restoring the Urban American Dream*, Stanford: Stanford University Press, 2014.

Wong, Cecilia, "Determining Factors for Local Economic Development", *Regional Studies*, Vol. 32, No. 8, 1998, pp. 707–20.

3. Quality of life and competitiveness

There has been work on competitiveness at both the national and the city level, and we can learn about its relationship with quality of life from each of these levels. As was the case with quality of life, the development of concern for competitiveness at the level of the city was preceded by that of the nation by several years. As early as 1983, a US government agency – the Office of Technology Assessment – issued a report on competitiveness in electronics, and two years later President Reagan appointed a Commission on Industrial Competitiveness. Members of the Senate and the House of Representatives in both parties also offered a variety of commissions and committees dedicated to national economic competitiveness. (Lodge and Crum, pp. 487–9) The proposals ranged from a national industrial strategy, to reform of tariff and tax laws, to investment in firms in emerging industries, to assistance to small business, and so forth, but there was nothing directed specifically towards cities or quality of life. The latter did get a brief mention at this time in Bruce Scott's discussion: "The degree of competitiveness is manifested in the whole fabric of society – from the educational system to the infrastructure to the quality of life – and affects decisions both by individuals and by firms to enter, remain, or exit". (Scott, p. 16) However, there is no discussion of exactly what is meant by quality of life, or of how it has an impact on a city's competitiveness. The objective of competitiveness was taken to be simply the achievement of a rising standard of living. The closest thing to a discussion of quality of life at this time is that with reference to the Quality of Work Life, in which the automobile companies and unions sought for a solution to the "Lordstown syndrome" when workers at the Chrysler plant in Lordstown, Ohio, on an impersonal and relatively automated production line, became alienated from the routine and drudgery of this work, and took drugs, with productivity and product quality suffering substantially. (Salter, Webber and Dyer, pp. 213–14) As was seen in Chapter 2, quality of life as an issue unto itself would have to wait at least a decade. As for the city, this, too, would have to wait as the discussion became dominated by Michael Porter's *The Competitive Advantage of Nations*, published in 1990.

At the heart of Porter's approach is his "strong conviction that the national environment does play a central role in the competitive success of firms". (Porter, p. xii) Porter does note that industrial clusters often locate in a specific city or region, and in these instances competitiveness is often based in local features, in which cases "the role of state and local governments is potentially" as great as or greater than that of the national government. Here, in 1990, he highlights the roles of university education, local regulations, research initiatives, local information, and infrastructure. (Porter, p. 622) This is a small window through which one can begin to discern quality of life elements. However, in his famous figure, The Determinants of National Advantage, there is little if any note of quality of life elements. (Porter, pp. 72 and 127) At this point his focus is entirely on industries and national governments. Paul Krugman rejected this approach stating diminishing competitiveness would lead a firm to declare bankruptcy, but that: "Countries, on the other hand, do not go out of business, they may be happy or unhappy with their economic performance, but they have no well-defined bottom line. As a result, the concept of national competitiveness is elusive". (Krugman, 1994, p. 34) And, more pointedly: "Competitiveness is a meaningless word when applied to national economies. And the obsession with competitiveness is both wrong and dangerous". (Krugman, 1997, p. 22) Certainly, he would say the same about cities.

Clearly, one can say that cities do not go out of business, although many of their residents would not agree. If we compare the recent activity of Youngstown, Ohio with Portland, Oregon, or Detroit, Michigan with Austin, Texas, it is clear that something important is going on. Some cities do in fact "go out of business" while others experience impressive growth in income, population, economic activity and quality of life. In fact, since 2010, 69 US cities have filed for bankruptcy, even if only for a municipal entity such as a water treatment facility, but there have been nine bankruptcies by municipalities themselves, including (most famously) Detroit, San Bernardino and Stockton. So the picture is not as clear cut as Krugman would have us believe.

Shortly after Porter's *Competitive Advantage of Nations*, scholars began to focus on the competitive advantage of cities, or rather urban competitiveness. To see how far they have come from the skepticism of Porter and Krugman, we can refer to the work of Jordi Borja and Manuel Castells. For them, the competitiveness of some spatial entity – nation, region or city – depends on: "the efficient functioning of the regional-urban system …, membership of global-type communications systems …, skilled human resource …, public backing of the economic and social agents …, representative, effective and transparent political institutions …, drawing up a city or region project …, and governability of the territory based on social cohesion and civic participation". This is far from the competitiveness of a firm with its technology, workers, plant and equipment and marketing strategy, and represents a new way of looking at the relationship between the city and competitiveness. Interestingly, they argue that: "The large cities are the multinationals of the twenty-first century. They are a place of encounter and of going beyond state policies and business initiatives". (Borja and Castells, pp. 119 and 123) For them, sustainability is linked with both competitiveness and quality of life, and "there is no insuperable contradiction between competitiveness and social integration, between growth and quality of living. In the long run, the most competitive cities in international terms are those offering the best quality of life to their inhabitants". (Borja and Castells, p. 23) This takes us far beyond both Porter and Krugman, and to a structured examination, in this regard, of the city itself.

THE FOCUS ON THE CITY

Thus, up through Porter there is little or no mention of either the city or quality of life in the literature on competitiveness until writers such as Borja and Castells, in the 1990s. However, even before them, there were others who were taking note of cities. Most emphatic was the Eurocities Movement when it declared, in its conference document in 1989, that "Now is the time for the cities!". (Eurocities) Eurocities was founded in 1986 by the mayors of Barcelona, Birmingham, Frankfurt, Milan and Rotterdam. By 1989 membership had grown to 14 and today it consists of 140 of the largest cities in 39 European countries. The organization has six thematic forums and works closely on urban related policies with the European Union. Five years later, in 1994, the OECD and the Government of Australia held a conference in Melbourne on the subject of Cities and the New Global Economy. About 80 presentations were offered by scholars such as: Ed Glaeser, Peter Hall, Klaus Kuentzmann, Charles Landry, Michael Parkinson, Rémy Prud'homme, and Saskia Sassen. This conference and the Eurocities manifesto stimulated an increase in the attention that was given to the city as an actor in a competitive world economy. Not simply as an entity to which things happened and that responded reactively to them, but as an agent that initiated policies and actions and that attempted to chart its own economic course. It was also interesting to note that in 1999 *Urban Studies* issued its "Review Issue: Competitive Cities".

About this same time some writers began to focus on cities as increasingly independent actors in a way that supported the assertion of Eurocities. This is a large area of literature and it will suffice to mention just two of these analyses. In 1991, Saskia Sassen asked: "Are New York, London and Tokyo actually part of two distinct hierarchies, one nation-based and the other involving a global network of cities? ... (M)ajor tension derives from the fact that much of the new growth rests on a weakening of the nation state". (Sassen pp. 327–9) Peter Taylor suggested that: "Bringing globalization into the argument can now be read as a 'freeing' of cities from containerization imposed by state ... These cities and other world cities operate through a world city network, ... cities that are being fundamentally liberated from entrapment within territories". (Taylor, pp. 200–201) He concluded that "we can no longer assume a general mutuality of interests between state and city". (Taylor, 1995, p. 60)

This does not represent a liberation of cities from national constraints as much as a recognition of a changed relationship between urban and national entities. More recently, Bruce Katz and Jennifer Bradley wrote, "The tectonic plates of power and responsibility are shifting, ... Power is devolving to the places and people who are closest to the ground and oriented toward collaborative action. The metropolitan revolution has only one logical conclusion: the inversion of the hierarchy of power in the United States". (Katz and Bradley, p. 5)

At the sub-national level there has been a great deal of metropolitan organization for the purposes of analyzing their condition in the national and international economies, of formulating new policies that can advance their efforts to ameliorate the standard urban problems relating to housing, transportation, poverty, economic competitiveness, education, and integrating young people into the society and its economy, sharing their experiences (both successes and failures), and increasing their political clout. Today there are estimated to be about 300 city networks in which city-to-city cooperation is situated. (Pipa and Bouchet, p. 2) In the US there are: (1) The National League of Cities, established in 1924, which now has over 1,900 member cities, towns and municipalities. There are similar organizations for governors, counties, state governments, state legislatures, and an International City/County Management Association. (2) The United States Conference of Mayors, founded in 1932, with over a membership of 1,400 cities with populations in excess of 30,000. This group adds immigration and international affairs to the issues treated by the NLC. These have become very important organizations for representatives of all levels of sub-national government to coordinate efforts and initiatives, and to lobby in Washington on issues of importance to them and to their residents. Needless to say, almost all nations have developed similar activist organizations, and their work has significantly transformed the situation of the cities and worked to the benefit of citizens, as well as establishing global networks of cities. Eurocities was pre-dated by these other city organizations, but it was more assertive and even aggressive in its message to national and international levels of government.

Shortly after Porter's *Competitive Advantage of Nations*, scholars began to focus on the competitive advantage of cities, or rather urban competitiveness. To see how far they have come from the skepticism of Porter and Krugman we can review some of the work of scholars on the competitiveness of cities. An interesting introduction to this literature is a study by Daniel Naud and Rémy Tremblay in which they compare the results of five rankings of cities that are highly placed for their knowledge economies. Three institutes – AEA/ NASDQ, University of Minnesota, and Brookings – ranked cities according to the number of employees in high technology, Milken used a Tech Pole index, and Progressive Policy used an index of the new economy. To examine the details of each of these would take us far afield, and we will just look at the results. The number of cities ranged from 14 (Bookings) to 315 (Milken), while the other three included 30, 50 and 60 cities. Naud and Tremblay compared the rankings of either 14 cities, for Brookings, or 17 for the others. San Jose was ranked #1 in three studies, #8 in one and not ranked in the fifth; Austin was ranked in three studies at #16, #2 and #8; Atlanta was ranked #10, #7, #11, #6 and #5; and Seattle was ranked #5, #13, #3, #15 and #7. The University of Minnesota included in its index aeronautics, pharmaceuticals, biotechnology and services; AEA and NASDAQ concentrated on R and D and production of informatics materials. The lesson here is that one has to be alert to exactly what criteria are used for the ranking.

We can examine several of the competitiveness rankings of cities chronologically from the earliest in the 1990s to the very latest done in the 2010s. Paul L. Knox put major cities in the context of a world structure in 1995 when he noted that one could purchase a French or German car but not be sure how much of it was the product of that country and how much of it was produced somewhere else in a plant in Asia or North America. Globalization had its impacts on production of goods and services, and it also had its impact on urban economies in a system of world cities that is dominated by urban centers of finance, corporate head offices, and information processing. They had become the command or decision centers for the global economy, and every other city had to develop a relationship with this structure. (Knox, pp. 6–7)

John Friedmann, in that same book, suggests an ordering of world cities based on what he refers to as "spatial articulations", of which there are four. The Global financial articulations consist of London, New York and Tokyo, global centers of banking and finance. The Multinational articulations cities are Miami, Los Angeles, Frankfurt, Amsterdam and Singapore. Each of these cities is the dominant economic center of a geographic region or continent. Important national articulations, of which there are seven, are cities such as Paris, Mexico City and Seoul that have a dominant position in an important nation. Finally, subnational/regional articulations, of which there are 15, are cities such as Osaka-Kobe, Chicago, Toronto and Milan that are dominant in a major part of a national economy – they may be thought of as "second cities". He writes that: "We must understand global cities in relation to their respective peripheries." (Friedmann, p. 42)

Knox finds Friedmann's loose structure of articulations to be too structured and he counters that "a hierarchical classification of world cities is less and less satisfactory". He offers a classification of world cities that consists of three primary functions: (1) transnational business – the number of Fortune 500 head offices in each metro area, (2) international affairs – number of NGOs and IGOs located in the city, and (3) cultural centrality – the ratio of the city's population and that of the next largest in the nation. (Knox, pp. 9–10) His classification gives us: Brussels and Paris as having the highest score on international affairs, Tokyo and New York as culturally central, with London between the two, and with 25 cities clustered with lower scores on both. Eight cities (Brussels, Paris, London, Tokyo Stockholm, Zurich, Amsterdam, and Madrid) rate highest in cultural centrality. This approach is descriptive, however, and does not get us far with regard to competitiveness, or to analysis of the details of each of the cities.

At the OECD conference in 1994 Peter Kresl and Balwant Singh reported on their study of competitiveness at the level of the city, 40 US cities, rather than of the nation. Their ranking was based on the growth in three variables for the period 1977–87: manufacturing value added, retail sales and business services. The cities were ranked and then 13 variables were used in a regression analysis to explain the ranking. (Kresl and Singh, 1994) Five years later, they published, in the *Urban Studies* issue on "Competitive Cities", a second study, this time of 24 US cities, using the same three variables for the period 1987–92. This time the data for the two periods was combined for the period 1977–92, and 16 variables were used to explain the ranking. (Kresl and Singh, 1999) A third, and final, study was published, again in *Urban Studies*, in 2012, for 23 US cities. (Kresl and Singh, 2012) In this study cities were also clustered by geographic region and it was then possible to examine how the Pacific coast, the North east, the South, the Center, and the Industrial triangle gained or lost competitiveness in relation to the other regions over this period of time. Over the three periods studied, a total of 20 explanatory variables were used and it was then possible to compare some variables, which were designated "hard", with others, which were "soft". Over time it was clear that the "hard" determinants, such as plant and equipment, per capita income and population growth, became less important as determinants of competitiveness than the "soft" determinants, such as healthcare, public security, and amenities – all quality of life aspects.

A related issue to national competitiveness is that of urban competitiveness on a world scale. This has always seemed to be extremely difficult when one just considers getting accurate data for scores of variables for hundreds of cities, but we can review the accomplishments of two scholars who have done just this. The first is Ni Pengfei, of the Chinese Academy of Social Sciences in Beijing. Ni has a staff of colleagues and students who have command of many languages so they can get into national statistical sources around the world. His first work, however, was *Urban Competitiveness of China* and evaluated the competitiveness of 47 of the country's largest cities. He also examined the four major economic regions of China, Yangtze Delta (Shanghai), Pearl Delta (Hong Kong), the Bohai Sea Basin (Beijing), and Central and West China. He used 13 major variables and broke them into two categories, hard variables and soft variables. The hard included, among other things, aspects of the labor force, finance and capital, science and technology, enterprises and infrastructure; the soft included, among other things, social order social consciousness, culture system, and economic openness. (Ni, pp. 22–37) Ni then does a fuzzy curve analysis of the data, to give a ranking of the 47 cities by their competitiveness. Later in the book, he does this exercise for 200 cities in China, and a briefer analysis of 110 cities from around the world. (Ni, pp. 88–9, and 190–197; and Ni and Kresl, pp. 18–21)

Ni then published a series of studies annually that presented the results of his analysis, using a similar methodology for world cities. The first in this series was published in 2007–08 and continues until today. The report gave a perfunctory ranking of 500 cities, and a more detailed analysis of the top 150, using 50 variables. Recent issues have included research reports by scholars prominent in urban competitiveness analysis.

Another project that analyses competitiveness is by Robert Huggins. In his *The Global Competitiveness of Regions*, he presents his World Competitiveness Index of Regions. His regions are urban regions and among the 546 included are Tokyo, Stockholm, San Jose-Sunnyvale-Santa Clara, Norway, and Queensland. Many would be considered to be analogous to the US Metropolitan Statistical Area, with anomalies such as Norway and Queensland. (Huggins, Izushi, Prokop and Thompson, ch. 3) The regions are evaluated on the basis of 19 variables such as knowledge capital in areas such as: (1) IT, biotechnology, Hi-tech services, and private equity, (2) knowledge capital based on traditional manufacturing such as manufacturing employment, managers per 1,000 employees, and R and D performed by government and by business, (3) labor productivity, labor productivity earnings and unemployment, and (4) education expenditures on various levels of instruction, and internet hosts and broadband access. What is refreshing in this work is the discussion of the difficulty in getting good data from so many city-regions and countries. Different entities use different definitions or indicators, the level of the "region" in individual nations may differ, and in many instances data may be estimated using the best techniques possible.

Huggins, et al., are able to compare ranking results for two different years, 2008 and 2014, using an earlier but more limited number of 145 (city) regions. This is something that Kresl and Singh were also able to do with data and rankings from their three studies. One of the interesting findings is that one might expect the regions with the most significant increase in their ranking would be regions in the Global South, but, although Ulsan (Korea), Shanghai and Beijing are in this group, 13 of the top 16 were city regions in Europe. Also interesting is the fact that of the 20 city regions that declined in ranking the most, with the exception of Manitoba, Iceland, and Shiga and Kanagawa in Japan, the other 16 were all located in the US. They also find that between 2008 and 2014 city regions in the US declined from 70 percent of the total to just 34 percent, Europe was steady at 27 percent, but that those in East Asia,

Australia and Russia increased by 3 percent to 36 percent. (Huggins, et al., pp. 38–41)

It is interesting to note that in the Huggins ranking system there is no place for variables that relate to quality of life or to amenities. However, in Ni's analysis there are seven categories of competitiveness variables, one of which is Living Environment, and in this variable one finds culture and entertainment, dining and restaurant, shopping environment, social (public) security, and natural environment and environmental quality – all of which are classified as quality of life or amenities variables. In the human resource category are health, literacy, education development, and status of talent, each of which could also be included in quality of life or amenities. So Ni's study of urban competitiveness is closer to the area of interest of this book.

Ranking cities has become a growth industry in recent years, and we will not venture forth into this area. But some of this work can be examined in Kresl's book *Urban Competitiveness*. (Kresl, ch. 7)

THE FOCUS ON QUALITY OF LIFE

In this first half of the book we are examining what quality of life can do for a city's economy – that is, the consequences of a certain character of quality of life. We have already looked at the relationship between quality of life and competitiveness, that is, how quality of life has been seen to enhance a city's competitiveness. As we saw, not all evaluations include quality of life as a determinant of urban competitiveness, however several place it at the center of explanatory variables. In this section we will examine its impact on the nature and structure of a city's economy.

Quality of life began to get some attention as early as 1987, when Leo Klassen noted that for highly skilled workers in the Alpine region cultural events and major airports were as important as Alpine sports, and the "the interests of the employee are becoming the decisive factor in the choice of location". (Klassen p. 253) More to the point, William Lever wrote in 1989, with regards to competitiveness and European cities, that: "A successful city, however, will not be judged solely by its rate of economic growth or profitability. Amongst a multiplicity of criteria for judging success will be distributional issues, economic development (rather than mere growth), sustainability and quality of life". (Lever, p. 1030) However, when he examines several studies of urban competitiveness in Europe quality of life never comes up as a determinant. Shortly thereafter, in 1993, Neil Pierce highlighted the "symbiotic relationship between arts, culture, healthcare, crime, the environment and economic strength". (Pierce, p. 308) More recently, Jan van der Borg and Antonio Paolo Russo wrote that: "Households choose a city and a particular location according to the expected utility subject to a set of constraints. As lifestyles evolve and available income grows, these come to include 'quality of life' as well as access to markets commodities and jobs". (van der Borg and Russo, p. 16) They saw culture as both a quality of life phenomenon and an economic activity, to be essentially an urban phenomenon, and that the demand for it grows as lifestyles change and populations age with seniors having more leisure time, educational attainment increases, participation becomes more diversified, and urbanization increases and reinforces the link between it and the supply of culture. Thus, over the years the causal relationship between quality of life and economic activity has intensified.

An alternative view is offered by Enrico Moretti who tried to separate fact from fable with regard to the impact of quality of life on a competitive economy. He wrote of two approaches to developing an urban economy. (Moretti, pp. 188–93) The first is to attract employers, with tax breaks and other incentives in hopes that the presence of companies will attract workers. The second is to attract workers as an inducement for companies to establish facilities. The trick is to make the city attractive to the desired category of workers by developing an attractive quality of life. He commented that before Microsoft and Amazon in Seattle there was Jimi Hendrix; in Austin, before Michael Bell's computer there was Willie Nelson. That is to say, there was an attractive dynamic local music and social scene that attracted young workers. This may be truer for Austin than it was for Seattle. Before there were Microsoft and Amazon, there was the Boeing Bust of 1969–71 when the market for commercial aircraft tanked. Boeing laid off thousands of tech workers and engineers. These workers liked the, perhaps mythical, Seattle life-style of catching salmon in the morning and then skiing in the afternoon, and did not want to leave for a job elsewhere. So they stayed in Seattle and used their knowledge and skills to do what engineers do – they built things, such as computers and software. In this counterview, it was after this, perhaps unique situation, that Seattle "took off" into its current configuration.

But it is not necessary to focus solely on large cities. Witold Rybczynski writes that: "Not so long ago, big cities were easily distinguished from small towns and rural areas by their quality of life ... Today, the nature of suburbs and exurbs makes it difficult to define exactly where the city stops and the countryside begins". (Rybczynski, p. 166) He refers to Irving Kristol's notion that "whether this life be lived in a central city or a suburb or a small city ... it is *life in an urban civilization*". (Kristol, p. 31) This notion of the "urban civilization" is very important because it defines the urban setting as not being different from suburban or rural communities – they are all urban to Kristol in an important sense. What is developed for the large city, mass marketing, telecommunications, entertainment, the internet, television, FedEx, UPS, and shopping malls, are quickly made available to, and to some extent transform, smaller cities and towns. Wherever one lives today, one is immersed in an urban civilization.

As a city works to enhance its quality of life, it must make investments and provide other stimulants to the entities and areas of the economy that develop this sector. This entails efforts in the areas of sports, recreation, culture, neighborhoods, paths and walkways, restaurant and bar districts, club areas, K-12 education, libraries, and lecture spaces. Many of these facilities and areas are part of the natural life of a city, perhaps requiring only some imaginative changes in zoning, but there are several that require extraordinary planning and expenditure on the part of the city government. Lecture programs, some cultural activities, and some sports are provided by universities and colleges throughout the city. We will examine two of these areas, professional sports and cultural institutions.

Sports stadia have been features of US cities, large and small, since before the Civil War. This includes baseball, football, basketball, and hockey, all of which can be played on a simple field of grassy land or a frozen pond. To discuss all of these would take us off the track, so we can use baseball as a proxy for the others. This can be reviewed by using Paul Goldberger's wonderful book, *Ballpark, Baseball in the American City.* (Goldberger) In New York City it was difficult to find a suitable space for a ball park, but a solution was found across the Hudson in Elysian Fields in Hoboken in 1845. This was a simple open field with no walls or bleachers. As the game became more popular, cities began to see value in ball parks. They cost money and took up city land but they soon became business ventures, with investors and ticket sales, and with customers for everything from street cars and trains to bars and food sellers at the park and nearby restaurants. Fans identified with the team and the team and the city became identified with each other. Before the 19th century had come to its end, ball parks began to take on the shape, structure, and appearance of modern ball parks. The early ones, in the 1880s such as Fenway Park in Boston, Wrigley Field in Chicago, and Ebbets Field in Brooklyn were steel and concrete parks in the city close to the working people who would walk to the game. Baseball was very popular and having a major park in one of the two leagues, American and National, was a prestige thing for any city.

As the 20th century progressed, baseball parks evolved from inner city neighborhood phenomena to grand spaces for the ball park and acres and acres of parking for those who had to drive to a park in Chavez Ravine, and it was a long drive for everyone, in a city that celebrated the car. For Goldberger the epitome of ball park construction was that of Oriole Park at Camden Yards, in Baltimore. The leaders of the promoters of Camden Yards referred to Jane Jacobs and her respect for pedestrian-oriented older cities in designing the project, and the park actually is in down-town Baltimore with easy access for all. He quotes a writer for *Sports Illustrated* as commenting that Camden Yards is "a real ballpark built into a real downtown of a real city". (Goldberger, p. 218) After Camden Yards new ball parks were built in Los Angeles, Kansas City, Arlington (Texas), Denver, Cleveland, Phoenix, Seattle, Houston, San Francisco, and Milwaukee.

It is clear that cities want to have major sports stadia, for as many sports as they can. The economic impact is usually very substantial, and varies from city to city.

Rather than getting too deeply into the finances of this, I will just look at the consequences of shutting down professional sports because of the coronavirus this year. In total, US sports amount to $100 billion, and the virus shutdown will cause the cities that host them $12 billion. (AFP) Major League Baseball without spectators for half a season would result in $2 billion in lost revenues. Professional sports would lose $5 billion in revenues. In addition, 3 million jobs depend upon sports. So this is a major financial benefit to participating cities. The stadia also have executive boxes that are popular with corporations resident in the city, and the publicity the city gets is of enormous value. The conclusion must be that sports have a powerful impact on city revenues.

Museums and concert halls are also of great economic benefit to a city. This can be demonstrated with an anecdote rather than data. When United Airlines was searching for a new headquarter city, better situated between Asia and Europe than Seattle for 500 of its top executives, it made a final selection between Denver, Dallas and Chicago. The search team visited Denver and was given a barbeque dinner and an introduction to John Ellway, quarterback to the Denver Broncos. Then in Dallas there was a Mariachi bank and a Mexican buffet. Finally, in Chicago the event was in the Art Institute, with music by members of the Chicago Symphony, and perhaps under Seurat's *Sunday on La Grande Jatte*. Thinking that they would have occasion to entertain senior executives from Japan Air and Lufthansa, the team chose Chicago.

The major cities of the world all have impressive collections of cultural institutions – symphony orchestras, operas, theaters, museums, and dance companies. Decades ago, James Heilbrun identified "Art and Culture as Central Place Functions". (Heilbrun) They are, in a sense, the price of entry to the circle of important cities. In each of the studies done by Kresl and Singh culture institutions were a determinant of urban competitiveness. Although in the last study, for the years 1997–2002 the top ranked three cities, Miami, San Diego, and Phoenix, were ranked 21, 20 and 23 in culture, and the top ranked cities in culture, New York, San Francisco and Boston, ranked 6, 19 and 13 in competitiveness. Each of the cities, it must be added, did have a substantial collection of cultural institutions and venues. For the economy as a whole, Heilbrun and Charles Gray estimated that the total expenditures on the arts sector, in 1990, amounted to $7.3 billion. (Heilbrun and Gray, p. 8)

For a major cultural center, the economic impacts can be substantial. New York City publishes data about the art, culture and creative economy. In 2017, total employment in this sector came to 231,000, and wages amounted to just over $30 billion, with an average wage of just over $100,000. There were 15,000 establishments – galleries, concert hall, theaters, museums, and so forth. Total economic activity for that year amounted to $110 billion, or 13 percent of the total economy. (Stringer) This is hardly typical for a US city, as New York City activity amounts to 12 percent of this sector for the entire US, but the sector is equally important for other cities such as Los Angeles, San Francisco, Chicago and Boston, to name only the most important. Even the smaller cities have musical performance spaces, some galleries and theaters, and other cultural venues. In the Kresl and Ietri examination of smaller cities in the US and Europe, they found that the most competitive ones always had a complex of these institutions, certainly those with a university or college. (Kresl and Ietri, pp. 39–40)

In Europe, the concerns and the impacts are similar, but with an added dimension: "Towns and regions where the economy is weak are at risk of not being able to afford the investment necessary to maintain their heritage. If that heritage crumbles (perhaps literally) then assets of potential economic value are lost. The sense of identity, an intangible but important force of cohesion, is also likely to be undermined". Culture is seen here as an integral element in the maintenance of the identity and political integrity of the European Union. Culture sector clusters are thusly important for cohesion and revenues from tourists, but also as vital elements "in creating places with the qualities that attract highly skilled workers and specialized industries, not least those with a key role in the knowledge economy". (ESPON, pp. 81–2) Even in the cultural sector, quality of life is seen as a powerful element in a city's competitiveness.

THE DOWNSIDE OF QUALITY OF LIFE

A high level of quality of life will be very attractive to the mobile, talented workers who have been the central focus of this book. The higher the quality of life the more attractive the city will be to this cohort of the work force. In order to attract this group the city will, as has been noted, work to put in place the elements of life that this group finds attractive, and objectively we must agree that the quality of the place will be enhanced by investments in cultural institutions, recreation facilities, public education, the healthcare system, public security, congenial neighborhoods, and so forth. But we must also take note of the negative externalities that attach to these desirable features of urban life. The high-tech economy we create with its talented and highly paid workers, the gentrification of previously working class and ethnic neighborhoods, and the exorbitantly wealthy entrepreneurial and owner class – the top 5 percent of the income distribution, concomitantly create the elements that are causing so much turmoil and alienation among those who are not in these fortunate classes. Case and Deaton write eloquently about the threats to life of this "other half" of the population (see Chapter 1), as does Desmond with regard to their eviction from home and neighborhood (see Chapter 2). Thus we must ask the question posed, in Chapter 2, by Eugene McCann – quality of life for whom? (McCann, p. 1927)

Hence there is a dynamic element in the notion of a high quality of life and we must recognize that the very concept itself evolves through the decades. We gave a précis of the development of the nature of the economy in Chapter 2, and noted the evolution from heavy manufacturing to services and retail to the knowledge economy. At each stage of development we can identify the elements in quality of life for the people who were involved in production at the time. During the first half of the 19th century working people had little time and little money for leisure activities and technological development had not done much to favor them. But during the last decades of that century and the first half of the 20th, as Robert Gordon informs us, many technological advances benefitted working people more than they ever had. Advances in transportation, communication, home appliances, electricity, and home conveniences brought much improvement to working people and their daily lives. Quality of life improvements involved things such as flush toilets, electric lighting, sewerage and refrigeration.

We might consider this to be of little consequence but it transformed their living from bare subsistence to a margin of leisure time. Working people began to take vacations in the summer, their children went to school and saw the prospect of doing something other than the occupations and work of their parents, and they had sufficient free time to attend the events in the new sports and cultural venues. The Great Depression brought much of this to a halt, but during the war production transformed the relation between labor and their work, unions grew, the standard of living increased and in a short time working people moved out of their traditional inner city ghettos and low income neighborhoods to locations that required access via the modern transportation of commuter trains and commuting by private car. The quality of life was transformed to include home ownership, the 40-hour working week, night school and other educational and skill development venues, and the possibility of advancement within the corporation for which they worked.

For these post-World War II workers, quality of life came to include leisure time, more time with the family, travel, access to improved healthcare, and gradual movement to the suburbs. Sadly, most of this was available almost exclusively to whites, while African Americans continued to live in red-lined districts of the city and not in more desirable "whites only" parts of town, and to be denied access to federal government FHA backed mortgages which made it virtually impossible for them to gain home ownership. This deprived them of the possibility to accumulate capital and wealth through a home, as was the case with whites. Several times since World War II American society seemed to be on the course of changing this situation fundamentally, but the effort has always failed. Perhaps today's protest movement will be more successful in enabling African Americans to create the relationship with white America that brings them the equality and access to all of the elements of contemporary quality of life they want.

The quality of life and its elements that are a feature of today's economy of knowledge and advanced technology are considerably different from those of post-World War II manufacturing and the services economy that evolved from it. Sadly, it has significant shortcomings to which we will now turn our attention. The new tech/knowledge economy has valorized aspects of city life and structures that have the power to attract and to retain the categories of worker who are central to this economic activity. There has been a strong preference for life in the city center, to the extent that firms located in smaller cities, such as Redmond and Bellevue, Washington, and several smaller cities in proximity to San Francisco, have arranged for fleets of company buses to take workers from the big cities in which they prefer to live to work in the corporate facilities across Lake Washington, for example. The influx of well-paid young workers into middle and low income housing areas in Seattle or San Francisco have greatly pushed up housing prices. This benefits lower income workers who own their home but forces out those who rent. This gentrification has substantially transformed the neighborhoods, the sorts of shops, restaurants and bars, and the social milieu in general. The "revitalization" of these neighborhoods also reconfigures the areas in which lower income workers are concentrated.

There have been many studies of the impacts of this change in people's lives, but that of Robert Putnam, in his *Our Kids*, will be sufficient to our needs. (Putnam, ch. 6) The central phenomenon to Putnam is a transition from income inequality to opportunity inequality. Income inequality has a static character while opportunity inequality is dynamic in nature. If people lack the capacity to change their situation in life and in the economy, there will be a substantial economic and social cost to the rest of society. If children grow up in a situation of residential segregation, poor quality schools, poor healthcare, unsafe neighborhoods, and income inequality or poverty, this will affect them for the rest of their lives. Lacking in education and skill development, they will be marginalized in the economy and the job market. Living in a dangerous neighborhood will affect almost all aspects of their life. They do not have role models to illustrate how they should act and behave. I had a student from a low income neighborhood as an advisee. In his sophomore year he joined a fraternity. To me, this seemed a bit strange for him, and when I asked him about it he said: "Professor Kresl, when I came to Bucknell my job opportunities were

Burger King or McDonald's. While I am here, I am going to learn how to dress like them, eat like them, talk like them, and act like them". Upon graduation he could imagine a job at a major financial institution or other business enterprise.

On the other side of it, those who are forced out of their neighborhood and end up in one that is far less salubrious become invisible to the wealthier residents of the same city. The result is a lack of interest in ending neighborhood segregation or in funding neighborhood improvements to parks, retail, grocery stores, improved access to transportation, and better funded schools. As a consequence, they become forgotten and their participation in the economy is not promoted. Many of these individuals are quite talented and capable of becoming high level workers. This amounts to a considerable loss of output, economic growth, creativity, and tax revenues, among other things, to the society as a whole. Estimates of the cost to society of this lack of investment in human capital through lack of social mobility range, for some cities, from 11 to 27 percent in economic growth over 10 years. (Putnam, pp. 232–3)

A loss of talented workers and an increased burden of social expenditures of this magnitude surely have a negative impact on the city's competitiveness vis à vis other cities which have taken on this integrative task. Jonathon Rose wrote that: "Cities are cauldrons of opportunity, but their overall happiness is dependent on the degree to which that opportunity is open to all their inhabitants". He offers several examples of students living in various neighborhoods and whose parents moved or did not move the family to a more opportunity-rich neighborhood and recounts the impact on future earnings of the student. His conclusion is: "So place matters". (Rose, pp. 351–61)

FINAL THOUGHTS ON QUALITY OF LIFE AND COMPETITIVENESS

In this chapter we have examined the relationship between urban competitiveness and quality of life, and also how the two concepts and the relationship between the two have changed in recent decades. The emergence of the awareness of the importance of competitiveness at the level of the city, and not just at that of the nation, has been a powerful development. If our attention is given to the welfare of individuals and to the economic viability of individual firms then the nation is not the most relevant level of society to study. Our attention must be on policies and development that will improve the immediate situation of individuals and firms; the nation is too distant an entity to be the primary area of focus for the attention of policymakers. The focus on the nation from Adam Smith's *Wealth of Nations* to Friedrich List's *National System of Political Economy* to Michael Porter's *The Competitive Advantage of Nations* has given way to the enormous outpouring of research on the competitiveness of cities. It is unclear whether there will be a shift in focus to something beyond the city as the primary context for economic entities and actors.

Analogously there has been an evolution in our understanding of the concept of the quality of life. Some of this was discussed in Chapter 2, and a little more than a bit of embellishment will be sufficient here. The concept of quality of life is, of course, directly linked to the individuals who are living in that place, at that time, and in the economy of that place and time. As the economy evolves so too, then, should the relevant conceptualization of quality of life. We have stressed the evolution of the dominant economy from manufacturing to retail and services to advanced technology and how this has altered our understanding of the most relevant notion of quality of life. The manufacturing worker, the office worker and the technology specialist all have different working and living situations, and this brings changes in leisure time activity, family life and concerns, geographic mobility, life past work (retirement), attendance at sports and/or cultural events, housing (location and type), demand for modes of transportation, telecommunications products and services, type of consumer goods, and demand for various urban spaces, among others. Any city that wants to take charge of its future development and the nature of its future economy will have to give serious attention to all of these aspects of quality of life. We have discussed most of this already and there is no need to belabor the relevant points further.

A final point could be made while we are examining evaluations of analyses of quality of life and urban competitiveness. Many of the critiques were offered at least a decade ago and even toward the end of the 20th century. Using data from a decade or thereabouts in the analysis, the authors were in effect examining an economy that existed between one and two decades earlier. Given the extent to which we have argued the economy of a period was marked by relationships, structures, stage of economic development, and quality of life elements, the critique offered was of an economy much of which was no longer of major importance. When city planners offer policies and proposals for investments, the economy in which they will be operative may, or rather probably will, be considerably different in nature than the one extant today. Hence, we must be careful when we use analysis of the economy that existed a decade or two earlier to propose actions for the next decade. Some features of a society and of an economy will endure but, given the pace of technological advancement, much will not.

REFERENCES

AFP, "Coronavirus US Sport Shutdown Will Cost $12 billion: Report", AFP, 1 May 2020.

Borja, Jordi and Manuel Castells, *Local and Global, Management of Cities in the Information Age*, London: Earthscan, 2010.

ESPON, *Territory Matters For Competitiveness and Cohesion*, Brussels: European Spatial Planning Observation Network, Autumn 2006.

Eurocities, *Documents and Subjects of Eurocities Conference*, Organizing Committee of the Eurocities Conference, Barcelona, Spain, 21–22 April 1989.

Friedmann, John, "Where we stand: a decade of world city research", in Paul L. Knox and Peter J. Taylor, (eds), *World Cities in a World-system*, Cambridge: Cambridge University Press, 1995.

Goldberger, Paul, *Ballpark, Baseball in the American City*, New York: Alfred A. Knopf, 2019.

Heilbrun, James, "Art and Culture as Central Place Functions", *Urban Studies*, Vol. 29, No. 2, 1992, pp. 205–15.

Heilbrun, James, and Charles M. Gray, *The Economics of Art and Culture, An American Perspective*, Cambridge: Cambridge University Press, 1993.

Huggins, Robert, Hiro Izushi, Daniel Prokop and Piers Thompson, *The Global Competitiveness of Regions*, London: Routledge, 2014.

Katz, Bruce J., and Jennifer Bradley, *The Metropolitan Revolution; How Cities and Metros are Fixing Our Broken Politics and Fragile Economy*, Washington: Brookings Institution Press, 2013.

Klaassen, Leo, "The Future of the Larger European towns", *Urban Studies*, Vol. 24, 1987, pp. 251–7.

Knox, Paul L., "World cities in a world-system", in Paul L. Knox and Peter J. Taylor, (eds), *World Cities in a World-system*, Cambridge: Cambridge University Press, 1995, pp. 1–20.

Kresl, Peter Karl, *Urban Competitiveness: Theory and Practice*, Abingdon: Routledge, 2015.

Kresl, Peter Karl and Daniele Ietri, *Smaller Cities in a World of Competitiveness*, Abingdon: Routledge, 2016.

Kresl, Peter Karl and Balwant Singh, "The Competitiveness of Cities: the United States", in the OECD and the Government of Australia, *Cities and the New Global Economy*, Canberra: Commonwealth of Australia, 1994.

Kresl, Peter Karl and Balwant Singh, "Competitiveness and US Metropolitan Centres", *Urban Studies*, Vol. 36, Nos. 4–5, May 1999, pp. 117–28.

Kresl, Peter Karl and Balwant Singh, "Urban Competitiveness and the Urban Economy: 24 Large US Metropolitan Areas", *Urban Studies*, Vol. 49, No. 2, February 2010, pp. 239–54.

Kristol, Irving, "Urban Civilization & Its Discontents", *Commentary*, Vol. 50, July 1970.

Krugman, Paul, "Competitiveness: A Dangerous Obsession", *Foreign Affairs*, Vol. 73, No. 2, 1994.

Krugman, Paul, *Pop Internationalism*, Cambridge: MIT Press, 1997.

Lever, William F., "Competitive Cities in Europe", *Urban Studies*, Vol. 36, Nos. 5–6, 1998, pp. 1029–44.

McCann, Eugene J., "'Best Places': Interurban Competition, Quality of Life and Popular Media Discourse", *Urban Studies*, Vol. 41, No. 10, September 2004, pp. 1909–29.

Moretti, Enrico, *The New Geography of Jobs*, New York: Houghton Mifflin Harcourt, Boston, 2012.

Naud, Daniel and Rémy Tremblay, "Discours sur la qualité de vie et la compétitivité des villes du savoir", in Diane-Gabrielle Tremblay and Rémy Tremblay, (eds), *La Compétitivité Urbaine à l'ère de la Nouvelle Économie*, Québec: Presses de l'Université du Québec, pp. 57–66, 2006.

Ni, Pengfei, *Urban Competitiveness of China*, Beijing: Social Sciences Academic Press, 2007.

Pierce, Neil, *Citistates: How urban America can Prosper in a Competitive World*, Washington: Seven Locks Press, 1993.

Pipa, Anthony F. and Max Bouchet, "How to Make the Most of City Diplomacy in the COVID-19 era", Brookings, 6 August 2020.

Porter, Michael E., *The Competitive Advantage of Nations*, New York: The Free Press, 1990.

Putnam, Robert, *Our Kids: The American Dream in Crisis*, New York: Simon and Schuster, 2015.

Rose, Jonathan F. P., *The Well-tempered City, What Modern Science, Ancient Civilizations, and Human Nature Teach Us About the Future of Urban Life*, New York: Harper Wave, 2016.

Rybczynski, Witold, *Makeshift Metropolis: Ideas about Cities*, New York: Scribner, 2010.

Salter, Malcolm S., Alan M. Weber and Davis Dyer, "U.S. competitiveness in global industries: lessons from the auto industry", in Bruce R. Scott and George C. Lodge, (eds), *U.S. Competitiveness in the World Economy*, Boston: Harvard Business School Press, pp. 185–229, 1985.

Sassen, Saskia, *The Global City: New York, London, Tokyo*, Princeton: Princeton University Press, 1991.

Scott, Bruce R., "U.S. competitiveness: concepts, performance, and implications", in Bruce R. Scott and George C. Lodge, (eds), U.S. *Competitiveness in the World Economy*, Boston: Harvard Business School Press, pp. 13–70, 1985.

Stringer, Scott M., *The Creative Economy: Art, Culture and Creativity in New York City*, New York: Office of the New York City Comptroller, 25 October 2019.

Taylor, Peter J., "World cities and territorial states: the rise and fall of their mutuality", in Paul L. Knox and Peter J. Taylor, (eds), *World Cities in a World-system*, Cambridge: Cambridge University Press, 1995.

Taylor, Peter J., *World City Network: A Global Urban Analysis*, Abingdon: Routledge, 2004.

van der Borg, Jan and Antonio Paolo Russo, *The Impacts of Culture on the Economic Development of Cities*, Rotterdam: Erasmus University, 2007.

4. Quality of life and the economy

Quality of life has become increasingly noticed and important as an issue for those who manage and plan city economies. In this chapter, we will examine the different ways in which this impact can be realized. The first, and most obvious, impact is that on the nature and the structure of a city's economy, and this is dependent upon the specific industries that can be linked to this set of elements of the quality of life, the impact this will have on the city's "brand", and its dynamism over time. Second, is the degrees of freedom the city will have in selecting a strategy from among the set of options that are available to it, rather than having to accept whatever comes its way. Third, is the impact quality of life can have on the city's long-term path of either advance or deterioration. An unattractive quality of life will generate an outflow of the population, a loss of spirit and confidence, and a secular decline, whereas a more attractive one will produce a robust confidence and optimism. Fourth, is the impact quality of life will have on the city's relationships with the national government and with other cities. A positive and confident city will be attractive as a partner to other similar cities. It is also the case that a city that is in decline will appeal to the national government for life-supporting transfers, while a city that is confident in its future will ask for support for items such as concert halls and transportation upgrades that will add to the attractiveness of the country as well as of the city. Finally, we will review the concept of degrowth, and how this can have an impact on a city's quality of life.

QUALITY OF LIFE AND THE STRUCTURE OF A CITY'S ECONOMY

A specific composition of quality of life will be suitable for a specific range of economic systems or of structures. When we consider the nature of the manufacturing, services and retail, and high technology economies, each will have a workforce, an image, a brand, a clientele, and aspirations that will be best suited to a specific composition of its most appropriate quality of life. City officials are certainly aware of this and must work continually to shape and reshape the package of quality of life elements so they accomplish what is expected. The quality of schooling, safety of neighborhoods, professional and neighborhood sports teams, access to affordable public transportation, availability of good recreational facilities, the vitality of the city's cultural institutions, the variety of restaurants and bars, and the city's age distribution all combine to create a suitable structure of the city's quality of life. This has to be aggressively promoted and advertised so the quality of life can achieve its desired objective – giving the city some influence on the structure of its economy.

Throughout this chapter we will have occasion to examine the link between a city's quality of life and various aspects of the city's options, its long-term path, and relations with other levels of government and other cities. Here we will explore the link between the city's economy and the most suitable quality of life. Charles Landry has written that: "A creative city is a place where people feel they can fulfil themselves, because there are opportunities. Things get done. It is a place where people can express their talents which are harnessed, exploited and promoted for the common good". This situation serves to attract other valuable skills and talents to the city. (Landry, p. 521) This notion can certainly be expanded to be applicable to all types of economy. Manufacturing has always required skilled labor, in addition to less developed muscle work, and employers sought to encourage these skilled workers to migrate to their factory town(s). Railroad and shipping companies advertised aggressively to encourage skilled workers to migrate to North American agricultural land, both in the US and in Canada, and to bustling large metropolitan centers such as New York, Chicago, Los Angeles, and Pittsburgh, with their booming factories. These places all had, or quickly developed, substantial ethnic neighborhoods with the appropriate religions and educational institutions, food stores, affordable housing, personal care facilities for women's hair and for health services, financial institutions that could wire funds to the family "back home", and so forth. These were not the symbolically creative people to whom Landry referred, but they were very creative with the appropriate tools and mechanical devices. Today, we see the creativity of Cuban mechanics working on US cars that are 50–70 years old, with no imports of parts being possible.

The labor force in an economy of retail and services requires a substantially different set of quality of life elements. For one thing, for the first time leisure time and the need for after work spaces and facilities are demanded by the workforce. Many factory jobs took decades to get to a roughly 40-hour working week and that work was very physically demanding. Time off was for a beer with friends and then recuperation for the next working week. Retail and service sector workers had weekends free and were not physically affected by their work. Cinemas, music performance spaces, and, in some ethnic communities, opera houses and classical music concert halls were demanded. Much of the work required certain skills and education, but the city's high schools and community colleges were effective in providing literacy, numeracy and the required basic skills. Large department stores developed in all cities, as noted in Chapter 2. Clearly, neither manufacturing workers nor retail and service workers would find the quality of life elements desired by the other group to be very attractive.

Finally, we get to Landry's targeted group, the creative workforce, for which "conditions need to be created for people to think, plan and act with imagination in harnessing opportunities or addressing seemingly intractable urban problems". (Landry, p. 517) Robert Reich identified three types of work: (1) routine production services (blue collar work), (2) in-person services (retail and services), (3) and symbolic–analytic services (Landry's creative workers). For Reich, the latter requires an extensive and finely articulated set of skills having to do with problem-identification and problem-solving, and they often work alone or in small and highly focused teams. (Reich, ch. 14) Landry stresses the need for "intercultural" places where there are a mixture of different cultures, attitudes and experiences: "There are places to meet, talk, mix, exchange and play. There is multicultural colour and diversity as this implies distinctiveness and varied insights". (Landry, p. 521) Much of the interaction is best done when there is a city district that is given over to this sort of economy, where individuals can meet by chance, stop for a coffee, and engage in the "exchange of tacit information" that is so important to the functioning of this economy. There is not much need for large department stores, ethnic bars, or even "affordable", that is to say low price, housing of the manufacturing or retail and services workforce. It is also true that much of the crucial "exchange of tacit information" occurs after midnight in suitable bars and other social spaces. (Currid, p. 6)

It is clear, then, that the three types of economies being discussed here have dramatically differing demands for quality of life. Each city's quality of life is suitable for a type of economy, and it is informative to consider the transition that had to take place for a city to make the transition from one economy to the next. Chicago is one city that had to restructure itself when it transformed from a manufacturing and meatpacking economy to retail and services. During the 20th century the city invested heavily in its cultural institutions to the point that they are among the most respected in the world. The institutions of the previous economy are not historical sites, such as the Pullman train car production community, or the stockyards. Some of the old steel mills are being converted to housing or to parks. Youngstown and Buffalo have been very slow to make their transition from manufacturing to something more current. However, Pittsburgh is a success story in which the country's major steel production center has abandoned, or been abandoned by, that industry and it has been replaced by healthcare and medical technology and by robotics, informatics and computer science. The city's neighborhoods, retail, entertainment, and social spaces have been transformed so they are congenial to this new and contemporary workforce. Both Chicago and Pittsburgh have to be considered as success stories.

QUALITY OF LIFE AND CITY OPTIONS

When the city leaders promote the quality of life they have worked to develop, they can start the process of restructuring or refocusing their local economy. They will of course, have to be clear as to what the current economy is, what is wrong with it, and where they want to take the city. Reshaping the quality of life will have to go hand-in-hand with the restructuring of the economy itself. It is often the case that a few individuals are crucial for the success of any urban economy. A century ago it was the Carnegies, Rockefellers, Fords, and others of their sort who were crucial for the success as manufacturing centers of Pittsburgh, Chicago, New York, Detroit, and other great cities; today in the tech economy it is David Packard, Steve Jobs, Bill Gates, Michael Dell (and scores of others, including those who have been called before Congressional committees to account for their actions in the market), Jeff Bezos (Amazon), Tim Cook (Apple), Mark Zuckerberg (Facebook), and Sundar Pichal (Google), as were their predecessors a century ago. (Romm) Today, the individual innovator and entrepreneur is of crucial importance, but he or she heads a team of thousands who are equally crucial for the realization of the vision of the leader and for the innovations that stem from that original idea. It is to this army of facilitators, large or small, that a specific quality of life is the *sine qua non*.

The innovator is not necessarily attracted to the place where the firm is initiated. Of the four tech leaders mentioned above, two were born where they established the firm – Steve Jobs in San Francisco and Bill Gates in Seattle – and two used the university they attended as the base: David Packard at Stanford University and Michael Dell at the University of Texas. But, when they moved to the expansion phase of the firms they established, then they had to be sure that the city in which the expansion would take place would have a quality of life that would be attractive to the skilled staff they wanted to hire. University cities do not require much attention as many of the staff will have graduated from those universities, and Silicon Valley/San Francisco, Seattle, and Austin are all known for their quality of life.

In examining the urban situation of today, Richard Florida has described the scene as "Winner take-all Urbanism". By this he references two distinct elements in this description. The first is the result of what Thomas Piketty highlighted when he noted that the return on capital had come to exceed the return on labor, or income. The result is the increase in the inequality of the distribution of income, with owners of capital capturing most or all of the increase in output, and with owners of labor having their income share remain constant. (Piketty, pp. 25–7) Florida concludes that a city's "most advantaged residents haul in the lion's share of the gains. Their less advantaged working and service classes are falling further behind". (Florida, p. 32) The rising inequality of income in the US was discussed above, in Chapter 2. Both agree that the distortion in the distribution of income is the dominance of the excess of rent accruing to owners of land and real estate, over the sidelining of wages that accrue to owners of labor and skill.

The second is the concentration of the gains from economic activity to a small number of "superstar" cities. Florida lists 20 of the cities, from New York and London to Moscow, "that have unique kinds of economies that are based on the most innovative and highest value-added industries, particularly finance, media, entertainment, and technology". (Florida, pp. 16–17) Superstardom is calculated by combining the rankings of five indices generated by other organizations, and is composed of: Economic Power, Financial Power, Global Competitiveness, Global Cities Index, and Quality of Life. The Quality of Life Index is based on the UN City Prosperity Index, which included five dimensions: productivity, infrastructure, quality of life, equity and social inclusion, and environmental sustainability – quality of life seems to get lost in the middle of things.

One initiative that most city leaders have pursued is establishment of a "brand" for their city. Branding is widely used in the corporate world as a means of differentiating the firm from its competitors, letting potential customers know what the firm can offer them, reminding the staff of the firm what their principal objectives and activities must be, and establishing a base for future developments. As written by two specialists in place brand management, Gregory Ashworth and Mihalis Kavaratzis, branding must be: "a wide-ranging strategic choice that includes the place's vision, the involvement and motivation of all the place's internal and external customers and users and its economic, social and cultural consequences". (Ashworth and Kavaratzis, p. 238)

The three tech cities identified above, Silicon Valley, Seattle, and Austin, all have well established brands, based on music, social life, competence, dynamism, residential allure, *joie de vivre*, and technical seriousness. This gives each city's leadership a degree of control over future evolution and direction of their city's economic development. While these three may not be among Florida's "winner take all" cities, they each have a dominant position in an area of economic activity in which they perform exceedingly well.

Both quality of life and branding have been important for cities that are attempting to refocus the specialization of their economy. There are many examples of this going back to Chicago at the end of the 19th century when grain trading, transportation and meat slaughtering gave way to manufacturing and financial services. At the end of the Civil War, Chicago had replaced Cincinnati as the Hog City, but this was quickly replaced by Second City, either the second city in population, or the city that followed the first when it was destroyed by the Great Fire of 1871. After the Columbian Exposition of

1893, "The City Beautiful" took hold. Carl Sandberg labeled it "City of big Shoulders" in 1914, and the "Windy City" was the most common popular reference. Mayor Richard Daly took charge of this process when he declared, in the 1950s, Chicago to be "The City that Works", referring either to its working class population of factory workers, or to the fact that under Daley things got done. Throughout 150 years the appellations that branded the city evolved in line with the nature of the city and its economy. The brand advertised to the world, or at least to the rest of the country, what Chicago was and what it aspired to become. Into each brand, one can read a reference to the city's reality that was linked to its quality of life – slaughter houses, factories, city of beauty and culture, and major metropolis. Some of the branding was pushed by the city leaders themselves, while some emanated from the sense of the residents, or of observers or admirers elsewhere.

QUALITY OF LIFE AND A CITY'S EXPANSION OR DETERIORATION

For cities to be stationary, rather than in relative movement, is rare when we examine rankings of cities over a period of years. As was made clear in Chapter 2, virtually all cities advance or regress over time in relation to other cities. There are always events, major or minor, that noticeably affect the city's position vis à vis other cities. An example is the financial crisis of 2008 when financial cities such as New York City were decimated, another would be a climate change that impacts agriculture such as a cold wave that destroyed the citrus crop in Florida, or a pandemic, as it powerfully destroys much of the world's production and the demand for both goods and services, as has happened in 2020. Hurricane Maria of 2017 destroyed much of Puerto Rico's economy and has left San Juan still trying to recover. On the other hand, ski cities such as Salt Lake City and Denver benefit greatly from several years of good snow fall. Obviously, quality of life is significantly affected in either direction depending on the event.

In this second half of the book, we are looking at what urban expansion or deterioration can do to the city's quality of life. That is, when New York City, Florida and San Juan deteriorated and Denver and Salt Lake City had good economies, what did this do to the city's quality of life? This is especially poignant today given the generalized negative impacts of the coronavirus pandemic. As is usually the case, we can see that there are short- and long-term effects on quality of life. We will examine the probable impacts of the virus on cities, or urban life, in Chapter 8, but for now we should state that while there may be some minor positive impacts for some people, on the whole it is a disaster all around. But the more interesting question for now is what are the impacts of secular advance or deterioration of a city's economic situation on quality of life? Things will be a bit clearer if we divide the city into two sectors: the sector that is involved in the expansion or contraction and the other sector that is not.

When the City is Expanding

An expanding city would appear to be in the best of situations. Employment high, incomes rising, population increasing, housing prices up, and good spirits all around. The community will be more attractive to high-end retailers, such as Whole Foods, oil and vinegar shops, wine stores with a much wider and higher quality selection, high end car dealerships, and so forth. So quality of life elements will be positive. This is true for a significant portion of the population. Another segment of residents will be virtually unaffected, if they have nothing to do with the expanding and competitive parts of the city's economy. If they are not in the housing market and own their house, they may be affected only by crowding at some leisure centres, traffic congestion, and other minor inconveniences. These groups should experience rising quality of life.

There is, however, another segment of the population that will be impacted negatively by upward pressure on housing rental prices, many of whom will be forced out of their residence to another that is less desirable, and perhaps more dangerous. In Pittsburgh, the expansion of medical technology, and of robotics and information security made the city attractive to younger workers in these fields. Many of them had been educated at the University of Pittsburgh or at Carnegie Mellon University, knew the city and knew where they wanted to live. This tended to be East Liberty and Lawrenceville, areas that had been working class districts for decades. The young "techies" took over the spaces and created the shops, bars and restaurants, and housing that suited them. Unfortunately, this resulted in many of the original residents having to relocate. Clearly, this did not work for them, so even in a rising city not all residents have an improved or improving quality of life.

When the City is Contracting

The fundamental reality of a contacting city is stress and fear. In cities such as Cleveland, Baltimore, Youngstown, and Utica, incomes fall, racial segregation increases, more people resort to scams and crime to gain income, stress increases because of the loss of employment, city tax revenues decline, and this results in less safe streets and neighborhoods, a decline of the city's cultural and recreational facilities, and a reduction in the quality of public education. A natural consequence is that population declines as jobs disappear and conditions worsen and people with any mobility at all pack up and go to greener pastures. This further reduces city tax revenues and disposable income

for retail, and for services such as restaurants and bars, hair salons, and entertainment. We are seeing these consequences in the life of the city during the
pandemic. Bankruptcies increase, social tensions are exacerbated, education is
threatened, the prospects for young people are diminished, and, in the words of
Chinua Achebe "Things Fall Apart".

On the other hand, housing prices do fall, and housing becomes available
as those who have mobility depart. Unfortunately, city officials often choose
not to spend available revenues to improve or at least maintain the wellbeing
of those who remain, but rather to cut services to the poor and spend whatever funds they have on attracting gentrifiers who will see financial gain in
upgrading deteriorated buildings. Peter Moskowitz found that in Detroit after
the declaration of bankruptcy in 2013, "the city's downtown, Midtown, and
Corktown neighborhoods have all experienced economic resurgence thanks to
corporations by pouring millions in to infrastructure and real estate projects,
but the rest of the city is crumbling … Gentrification is a system that places the
needs of capital (both in terms of city budget and in terms of real estate profits)
above the needs of people". (Moskowitz, pp. 7 and 9) Moskowitz is certainly
not the first to come to this conclusion, but reiterating it does make it unlikely
that lower income people will really gain from a city's decline. Clearly, quality
of life for all but the gentrifiers, or the unaffected, will deteriorate.

When the City is Stationary

The most obvious example of a city that does not expand or contract is the
university town. Witold Rybczynski puts it succinctly: "The college city is
different". (Rybczynski, p. 23) First, the university town is smaller – of course,
all large cities have universities but they are not university towns in any sense
of the term. These are cities such as Raleigh-Durham, Provo, Charlottesville,
on down to Burlington and even Lewisburg, where I live. They are largely
defined by the presence of the university. Second, they have the cultural life of
the university, good book stores, pleasant shopping areas, access to recreation,
and good cafes and restaurants. Third, in comparison with the large cities they
have affordable housing. He finished his essay by writing (p. 26): "Who would
have thought that that ivory tower would nurture that precious but rapidly
disappearing commodity: city life". Clearly, quality of life in a university city
or town is high and stabile, for most if not all of the residents.

The challenge to other, non-university towns that seem to be stationary is
the common experience that what gives the city its stability may in the longer
run not continue to be supportive. Resource-based city economies, based
on timber, furniture making, mining and metallurgy, and agriculture, to say
nothing of buggy makers and cities that are based on manufacturing a product
that is overtaken by technology – such as Kodak, in Rochester, New York,

or gas-powered sedans in Lordstown, Ohio, and other manufacturing cities throughout the industrial heartland, are all liable to eventual collapse. Clearly, the best strategy is one that works to diversify the city economy.

QUALITY OF LIFE AND RELATIONS WITH OTHER CITIES, AND NETWORKS, AND WITH THE NATIONAL GOVERNMENT

Cities in decline seek the advice of strategic planners and consultants, but they do not initiate collaborative relationships with other cities. If a city is in trouble, what does it have to offer other cities other than caution not to do what it has done? The city will be too focused on solving its own problems to conduct imaginative interaction with its counterparts – and, what does it have to offer them? Nonetheless, cities with problems do join large, generally focused associations of other cities for general support and inspiration.

No, it is cities that have charted a course for future development and have begun to progress in that direction that seek contact with other similar cities so as to share ideas about how to advance and how to resolve difficult issues, and to participate in groupings of cities that are in the midst of initiating new projects and probing in new directions. There are many examples of associations of cities that are nationally or continentally based, or are even globally based. In this section of the chapter we will examine several of them.

Nationally-based City Networks

In the US, the National League of Cities was founded in 1924, and has grown to a membership of almost 20,000 cities, towns and villages. Its principal issues include infrastructure, public safety, education and families. It has long lobbied the US Congress for policy and funding with regard to these issues. Its conferences bring together thousands of representatives of municipalities and it is quite different to the other smaller and more tightly focused groups. Its Center for Policy Solutions does work on sustainability, ecosystems innovation, leadership and universities. The US Conference of Mayors was established eight years later and limits membership to cities of at least a population of 30,000 – 1,407 in number. It does work on the usual set of urban issues, but perhaps its most useful role is that of getting mayors together to share ideas and information. This will be highlighted below in the comments of Chicago Mayor Rahm Emanuel. One of the principal current issues that has the attention of the Conference is the pressing need for federal funding of rather massive infrastructure projects. At their meetings they agree upon a set of policy resolutions which are then distributed to the President of the US and to the US Congress.

Most countries have national city organizations, usually of mayors, but often of policy people in the city government, such as Canada's Federation of Canadian Municipalities. They all have the same objectives as the US organizations, and express that same spirit of municipal activism in an environment of weak or distracted national governments.

Continentally-based City Networks

Several of these networks have been established in Asia and Africa, but the most renowned one is Eurocities. This was mentioned earlier in Chapter 3, when it was noted that it had grown to include 140 mayors in 39 countries. It has been very active in providing a place of discussion and polity formation for European mayors.

There had been little other than an occasional bi-national meeting of mayors from the US, Canada and Mexico, until the first North American Mayors Summit was held in Los Cabos, Baja California, Mexico, during 6–8 June 2019, with over 100 mayors in attendance. Several bi and multilateral city agreements on public policy and border issues were studied, and cross-border arrangements were agreed. The second conference will be held in Austin, Texas in 2020.

Asia is rich with mayors' associations, such as: (1) the Asian Mayors Forum, founded in 2008, to promote urban diplomacy and advocacy, and metro governance, (2) The Covenant of Asian Mayors for Climate and Energy which supports the Paris Agreement on Climate Change, (3) The ASEAN Mayors Forum which has, since 2011, advocated for the role of cities toward meeting the goals of the New Urban Agenda, the Paris Agreement of Climate Change, UN Sustainable Development Goals, and the Sendai Framework for Disaster Risk Reduction, and (4) The South-East Asian Mayor Conference, initiated this year, which devoted its attention to issues of education, investment, population growth and climate change. There is some inevitable overlapping of foci, but nonetheless these organizations do confirm the assertive role of mayors in public policy these days.

Globally-based City Networks

Other theme-based gatherings of mayors have been established on topics such as climate change and the environment. One, The Global Covenant of Mayors of Climate & Energy, has members on all continents and states that it represents the 10,000 cities in 138 countries that have agreed to undertake policy actions. It sees itself as an organization that can assist in the implementation of the Paris Climate Agreement. It has a board that includes mayors of major cities, such as the mayors or ex-mayors of Paris, New York, Accra, Seoul,

Pittsburgh, Lima, and Heidelberg. Another is the Global Mayors' Forum, established in 2005, which has sponsored an annual three-day conference on topics related to urban development including cooperation, development practices and urban planning. More specialized is the somewhat older (1979) International Association of Francophone Mayors. Its current policy objectives include the issue of decentralization, conflict prevention and regional development, and its membership consists of about 75 cities in Europe, North Africa and the Middle East.

There are, of course, many other specialized networks, but this gives one an idea of what they are and what they intend to do for their members.

The Mayorial Initiative

But it is not just through formal networks that cities interact, some are more entrepreneurial. A very valuable insight into this interchange is offered by the past Obama administration official and later mayor of Chicago, Rahm Emanuel. He has just written a book, *The Nation City*, in which he relates his interaction with other mayors in the pursuit of innovative policies that will benefit the residents of their cities. His basic point is that the responsibility and capacity to work on urban problems has devolved from national governments to mayors and their staff. Only they know what their city's problems actually are, how their city works and how the problems can be resolved through local action. He begins the chapter on "Horizontal Networks" by recounting his stroll along the Seine with Paris mayor Ann Hidalgo discussing restoration of city rivers and their banks. This motivated Emanuel to sponsor a conference on restoration of waterfronts, with 17 mayors from 11 countries on five continents participating. They shared ideas and successes and failures with no national government present – "It was just us". (Emanuel, p. 210) He and London mayor Sadiq Kahn signed a technology partnership agreement. He and Mayor Miquel Mancera of Mexico City established a truly functioning sister city agreement, one that included more than an exchange of school choruses. He celebrated the collegiality of the meeting of The US Conference of Mayors, at which he is able to interact with other mayors of large cities. Several of them have collaborated on programs for needs such as homeless people, and minimum wages – with "no federal plan – or federal resources ... There is no national plan. It's all left up to mayors and their cities". (Emanuel, pp. 217 and 220) This is a "new" model for urban policy to be proposed and enacted. Echoing the call of Eurocities, Emanuel seems to be declaring: "Now is the time of the mayors!"

Throughout, whether the program is for waterfront restoration, housing for the homeless, city beautification projects, lobbying for minimum wage increases, confronting climate change or providing recreation and safety for the city's youth, the actions of the mayors have overwhelmingly been to enhance the quality of life of the city's residents.

QUALITY OF LIFE AND DEGROWTH

In Chapter 2, we noted that there was much analysis to suggest that happiness and higher income are not necessarily positively related. More growth of GDP does not necessarily increase wellbeing, or quality of life. This was the conclusion of the UN World Happiness Report and much research on the distribution of income, and was in conformity with the Easterlin Paradox that de-links social richness and happiness. This being true, can we conclude that lowering income will lead to wellbeing, and to higher quality of life? This is one of the issues that is raised by the recently developing literature on "degrowth", to which we will now turn our attention.

The discussion begins with demonstration that quality of life cannot be said to be linked intrinsically to simply producing more goods and services. There is a diminishing marginal utility of additional goods and services, given that the trade-off is with more leisure time. So it should be immediately evident that we should, at some point, turn our back on the effort it takes to have more "stuff". What enters the scene, however, is the psychological need many of us have simply to have more in relation to other people. Several years ago, Ted Turner, who was ranked in the top five in the world in terms of wealth, made a donation of several billions to the United Nations. When interviewed about this, he said that the reduction in his personal wealth was of no significance to him, but for a short while he was terribly bothered by the fact that he dropped significantly in the rankings of the wealthiest individuals. There is only so much "stuff" you can handle and then it becomes redundant, and only your position vis à vis other individuals matters, wealthy or not, depending on the status of the individual. This casts the rationality of maintaining a system that produces as much as it can, mindlessly, into question.

Staffan Linder noted this 50 years ago, in his insightful *The Harried Leisure Class*. Linder argued that the leisure class is harried because every time one purchases some object – car, television, stereo, boat, tennis club membership – one has to devote hours to research so as to make the most satisfying purchase, then there is time required for periodic maintenance, and, finally, using it deprives one of using the other things one has purchased, or simply doing other things with one's time. He also finds that more goods are inimical to romantic courtship, to the art of the gourmet, and are diversionary to enjoying poetry, music, and introspection. (Linder, esp. ch. XII.) It is hard to avoid the conclusion that one's quality of life has been diminished. Reference is often made to an analogous comment by John M. Keynes that we have absolute needs and relative needs. The former are essential to survival but the latter, when we have advanced to a certain stage, will be "satisfied in the sense that we prefer to devote our further energies to non-economic purposes". (Keynes, p. 365) He, too, was a devotee of poetry, music, and introspection, as well as ballet.

There is not only some dissatisfaction with maximization of GDP, but with GDP itself. It has long been noted that GDP measures total economic activity, but it contains both "goods" and "bads", the latter of which count as output but that diminish welfare. An example is a forest fire, that requires the labor of hundreds or thousands of firefighters for an extended period of time, and then the reconstruction of the buildings and other structures that have been destroyed. Here it is difficult to argue that the forest fire adds to social welfare, rather it diminishes it, although the hours worked and the reconstruction material add to GDP. It has been suggested that a better measure would be the Genuine Progress Indicator (GPI), which is designed to measure wellbeing rather than just output. (Kubiszewski, et al., pp. 57–8) GPI adds to GDP 24 different components such as income distribution, cost of environment remediation, crime, and pollution, and adds items that have a positive impact on wellbeing, such as volunteering and household work. There are some dramatic divergences between GDP and GPI, as was noted in a study of 17 national economies from 1950 to 2010. The most striking case is that of Poland which had a steady GDP during the 1986–89 period of the collapse of communism, but a dramatic decline and then rebound of GPI during the same years. During the post-World War II years, both GDP and GPI for 17 major economies increased rather steadily; however from about 1980 onwards while GDP continued to rise, GPI became stationary. For all countries there is a strong correlation between the two measures, but after GDP attains a global per capita income level of $7,000, GPI slowly begins to decline from $4,250 to $3,750, while GDP continues to rise, and the correlation between GDP and GPI becomes negative.

John Cassidy refers to the comment of two 2019 Nobel Prize in economics winners, Abhijit Bannerjee and Esther Duflow, writing that "the misguided pursuit of economic growth since the Reagan-Thatcher revolution has contributed to a rise in inequality, mortality rates, and political polarization. When the benefits of growth are mainly captured by an elite, then, social disaster can result". (Cassidy, p. 25) Furthermore, others note that when incomes rise, individuals often choose to have fewer children as women enter the workforce, and try to reduce their time at work. This is a rejection of simply higher income leading to higher wellbeing, and results in a higher quality of life.

In its broadest sense, degrowth entails "less competition, large scale redistribution, sharing and reduction of excessive income". (Demaria, et al., p. 194) Degrowth seeks to scale down the material and energy utilized by economic activity and, indeed, to generate a reduction in overall economic activity. Akin to this is a "progressive distribution of existing income" as an element in a package of: a shorter work week, job guarantee and a living wage, and investment of public services such as public healthcare, education, affordable housing transportation, utilities, and recreation facilities. (Hickel, p. 57)

Jason Hickel sees the problem as beginning with the enclosures which can be seen as being rooted in 13th century England, when peasants were forced off common lands and obligated to farm a specific plot under the control of landed elites. Peasants lived a life that was static but provided subsistence. Gradually things such as cash taxes were assessed, which forced the peasants to produce a cash crop to earn cash for the tax. The result was the creation of an artificial scarcity that further obligated the peasants to be more subordinate to the land owner. It then became understood that to make the peasantry "industrious" they must be kept poor so as to further induce them to work. The Scottish merchant Patrick Coloquon wrote in 1800 that "without poverty, there could be no labor, there could be no riches, no refinement, no comfort, and no benefit to those who may be possessed of wealth". Poverty and hunger were then their fate until the Industrial Revolution when another form of exploitation was introduced. The final element for Hickel is the observation of the James Maitland, in 1804, that there is "an inverse correlation between 'private riches' and 'public wealth'". The contemporary manifestation of this is the "waves of privatization … of education, healthcare, transportation, libraries parks, swimming pools, water, even social security". (Hickel, pp. 60–63) This is clearly evocative of John Kenneth Galbraith's image of the family driving in a fully loaded car through a deteriorated city and on a potholed road to have a picnic "by a polluted stream and to on to spend the night at a park which is a menace to public health land morals". (Galbraith, p. 253) Hickel seeks to reverse the relationship and increase public wealth to the detriment of private riches.

The degrowth movement is closely linked to the green growth approach, although there is a tension between the two. There is an understanding that if we produce more then there will be more environmental damage through production processes, gas-driven vehicles, use of fossil fuels for generation of electricity, increased use of fertilizers, herbicides and pesticides, and urban sprawl. Far from being a fringe group interest, supporters include the World Bank, the OECD, many national governments, and, of course, the Paris Agreement on Climate Change. They, and the Global Commission on the Economy and Climate, argue that we can continue to have growth and prosperity through "the rapid technological innovation, sustainable infrastructure investment, and increased resource productivity". (Cassidy, p. 26) The issue of green growth became an issue in the US 2018 and 2020 elections with left-wing Democrats arguing for a Green New Deal, involving conversion of the US power generation to renewable zero-emission energy sources, such as solar and wind, upgrading existing building and expanding high-speed rail so as to reduce the need for commercial air travel.

The degrowth movement argues that by focusing on redistribution of income and supporting policies to increase availability of public goods, such as education, healthcare, etc., slower growth can generate gains in quality of life for the vast majority of the population, with Turner's loss of status being the only reduction in quality of life, if status can be considered an important element in quality of life, for the top 5 percent. The Green New Deal and other green economy supporters can argue that the reduction in greenhouse gases and other damage to the environment, in which we must all live, will also generate gains in quality of life. Both degrowth and Green New Deal types of policy initiatives are controversial and they must make their cases articulately, and quickly.

FINAL THOUGHTS

We began this chapter by noting that what we can consider to be quality of life is dependent on the nature of the economy in which the workforce will be functioning. Manufacturing, retail and services, and high tech economies all employ different and specific types of workers, and each type will have its own understanding of what elements in quality of life are important to them. Hence, quality of life is a flexible and evolving notion, and not at all fixed.

We then linked quality of life with the capacity of a city to select from a variety of options for its development. A century ago an entrepreneur or industrialist would attract the necessary labor simply by building a factory; today, the producer has to select a city that will be attractive to the desired high skilled and highly mobile labor force. Those desirable specialists will select an employer in accordance with the quality of life that city offers to the entire family. This has generated a genuine competition among cities for this key to long-term growth and development. Cities then "brand" themselves so as to advertise their essential quality/ies throughout the national, and international, economy. Branding can be used to advertise a city's current strengths and assets or to facilitate a change from a less desirable situation to one that is more advantageous and in line with the ambitions of the city leaders.

Quality of life is affected when a city is expanding or contracting, or just stationary. An expanding city economy would seem to be unambiguously advantageous; however in such situations aspects such as the housing market are affected in ways that disadvantage those who are not participants in the new economy. Low-income minorities tend to lose out when rents increase and they have to find new, and less desirable apartments to rent. Stationary cities such as university or college towns tend to have a quality of life that does not change and that is more satisfactory to virtually all residents of the city. Finally, cities that are contracting lose jobs, city services, retail outlets and safe streets. The only people who benefit are those who are able to gain access to funds to participate in the reconstruction of the deteriorated parts of the city. Little or none of this falls off the table for the benefit of the low-income residents who simply lose out due to their inability to move to a more salubrious neighborhood and employment, and simply suffer a loss of quality of life.

Finally, we examined the possibilities for cities to participate in a variety of multi-city networks and organizations that give them access to good information, and guidance through interaction with leaders, or staff, of other, perhaps, more successful cities. These organizations are at all levels from the national to the global. An important element in this is the increased activity of city mayors and the fact that these mayors are engaged in meeting collectively or one to one to discuss solutions to their urban problems and to coordinate efforts to influence national or global governing bodies. The primary desire of these mayors is the improvement of the quality of life of their constituents.

We have just finished a discussion of the impact on quality of life or the degrowth and environmental movements. This should be fresh in our minds, so we will not review this here.

REFERENCES

Achebe, Chinua, *Things Fall Apart*, New York: Knopf, 1992.
Ashworth, Gregory and Mihalis Kavaratzis, "Conclusion: in search of effective place brand management", in Gregory Ashworth and Mihalis Kavaratzis, (eds), *Towards Effective Place Brand Management: Branding European Cities and Regions*, Cheltenham, UK and Northampton, MA, USA: Edward Elgar, 2010.
Cassidy, John, "Steady State, Can we have Prosperity without Economic Growth?", *The New Yorker*, 10 February 2020, pp. 24–7.
Currid, Elizabeth, *The Warhol Economy: How Fashion, Art, and Music Drive New York City*, Princeton: Princeton University Press, 2007.
Demaria, Federico, Francois Schneider, Filka Sekulova and Joan Martinez-Alier, "What is Degrowth? From an Activist Slogan to a Social Movement", *Environmental Values*, Vol. 22, 2013, pp. 191–215.
Emanuel, Rahm, *The Nation City, Why Mayors are Now Running the World*, New York: Alfred A. Knopf, 2020.
Florida, Richard, *The New Urban Crisis*, New York: Basic Books, 2017.
Galbraith, John Kenneth, *The Affluent Society*, Boston: Houghton Mifflin Company, 1958.
Hickel, Jason, "Degrowth: A Theory of Radical Abundance", *Real-World Economics Review*, No. 9, pp. 54–68.
Keynes, John M., "Economic possibilities for our grandchildren (1930)", in John M. Keynes, *Essays in Persuasion*, New York: W. W. Norton, 1963.
Kubiszewski, Ida, Robert Costanza, Carol Franco, Philip Lawn, John Talbert, Tim Jackson and Camille Aylmer, "Beyond GDP: Measuring and Achieving Global Genuine Progress", *Ecological Economics*, Vol. 93, 2013, pp. 57–68.
Landry, Charles, "A roadmap for the creative city", in David Emanuel Andersson, Åke E. Andersson and Charlotta Mellander, (eds) *Handbook of Creative Cities*, Cheltenham, UK and Northampton, MA, USA: Edward Elgar, 2011.

Linder, Staffan B., *The Harried Leisure Class*, New York, Columbia University Press, 1970.

Moskowitz, Peter, *How to Kill a City: Gentrification, Inequality, and the Fight for the Neighborhood*, New York: Nation Books, 2017.

Piketty, Thomas, *Capital in the Twenty-first Century*, Cambridge: The Belknap Press of Harvard University Press, 2014.

Reich, Robert, *The Work of Nations*, New York: Vintage Books, 1992.

Romm, Tony, "Amazon, Apple, Facebook and Google Grilled on Capitol Hill over their Market Power", *New York Times*, 29 July 2020, p. 1.

Rybszynski, Witold, *Mysteries of the Mall, and Other Essays*, New York: Farrar, Straus and Giroux, 2015.

5. Demographics and quality of life

Issues of demography have become one of the most pressing for urban economies and for the quality of life of city residents. One of the features of demography that has caused so much difficulty, consternation and also hope for city
leaders is the fact that the elements of demography often have a dynamic of
their own. People procreate, die, move, age, express or alter their sexual orientation, commit themselves to one religion or the other, and relate to individuals
of other races with enthusiasm or with enmity. These elements will have their
impact(s) on the economy, the political life of the community, the image of
the city in other places, domestically or abroad, and on the quality of life of
the city's residents. Issues of migration and of various forms of discrimination
have become two of the most prominent issues of social policy throughout the
world today. In the US, discrimination against Blacks and other than hetero-
sexual individuals are on the evening news every day. While many see these as
national issues, all of those affected by discrimination do live in a city or town
or settlement, hence cities cannot avoid the necessity of enacting policies to
ameliorate or eradicate the consequences of the discrimination.

   But discrimination is not the only demographic issue that confronts cities
and their residents. Religious conviction, or lack thereof, has intensified as an
issue of contention during the Trump administration, and this has been blended
in with anti-Muslim sentiment and racial discrimination to generate a white
supremacy and "fascist"-based turmoil in many cities. Less turbulent has been
the issue of the aging of the population. Most economies are being confronted
by falling birth rates, later first pregnancy for most women, and restrictions
on the inflow of immigrants who, at least for the first generation, have larger
family sizes. An aging population is often presented as a rising cost to society,
but are there benefits as well as costs to an aging, or older, population? The
final issue of demography is the population size, and the rate and composition
of its growth. Is there some maximum sustainable rate of population growth?
Can the rate of population change be excessive, according to some criteria?
The tensions that arise from these issues can certainly cause a loss of quality
of life for those who have been attacked or discriminated against, while apparently affording some increase in quality of life to those whose lives are to some
degree freed of contact with these individuals or groups. It is arguable whether
there is a net gain in quality of life from this encounter.

Nonetheless, there are other non-confrontational elements of demography that we can study. Some researchers have argued that there is an optimal population size for a city and that quality of life will be maximized at this size and diminished at others. Growth of population, or its decline, and the pace of that change can generate social tensions that we should examine.

Based on the above, I have selected eight aspects of demography to study in this chapter and to relate to quality of life: (1) migration, (2) age distribution, (3) aging, (4) population growth rate, (5) population size, (6) religion, (7) racial composition and tension, and (8) sexual identification.

MIGRATION

Human societies always experience a certain degree of movement of population. A crisis in the production of food has generated substantial migrations from Ireland, Scandinavia, Central America and Africa in the 19th and 20th centuries. More recently, people have migrated due to the operation of drug trafficking and other criminal gangs and to the persecution of those who oppose a malevolent dictator in Latin America, Africa, Asia, and Eastern Europe, or are simply of the "wrong" religion. Another cause has been family unification, when a migrant to a country will invite other family members to join him or her. Finally, individuals who have gained an education and marketable skills often seek to migrate to another society where they, especially young women, can apply their skills and live a satisfying life. Economists generally support this movement because it is evidence of people freely choosing to enhance their quality of life, in that they are moving to realize a preferred set of public and private goods and services over a lesser set. (Glaeser, pp. 29–31)

Many nations to which migrants seek to move, such as Canada, have skills-based criteria for allowance of migrant entry. Points are awarded for the level of education achieved, languages spoken, work experience, employable skills, age, and financial resources. However, the US has always been a more welcoming nation, with some restrictions primarily on Asians at the turn of the 19th and 20th centuries, although this has been rather dramatically altered in the Trump administration. The US has generally valued their energy, enthusiasm, willingness to work and to contribute, and their willingness to help us to fill in the vast geographical space of the country.

It has overwhelmingly been the case that immigrants have benefitted materially and socially, although many immigrant groups have faced some resistance from labor in port cities where they would try to establish themselves. These reactions, from the Know-Nothing Party of 1840, the Chinese Exclusion Act of 1882, the Ku Klux Klan in the 1920s, to Trump's anti-Muslim act of 2017, have been widely discussed and we need not repeat these events here. For most, the improvement in quality of life has been immediate, and for the rest it has improved after a few years.

For the host country, in this case the US, its industrial expansion was fed by immigrant labor. Successive waves of immigration grew the population of the US from 3 million at its founding to 315 million today. In 1914, 71 percent of the labor force of Ford Motor Company were foreign born. (Freeman, p. 129) Thomas Piketty writes that one of the consequences of immigration for the US is that it tends to worsen the problem of income inequality because it has the tendency to postpone implementation of a "new type of regulation: a social state with progressive taxes on income and capital". This has the effect of increasing the development of "defensive nationalism and identity politics (that) will very likely grow stronger than ever". As with all such events, some residents will perceive that their quality of life has become diminished. (Piketty, p. 539)

Economists see a tension between the notion that all factors of production, capital, technology, ideas, and labor should be freely mobile so output can be maximized, and the restrictions that are placed on one of the factors, the migration of labor. (Milanovic, p. 147) Surely, if labor migrates and has a positive impact on national GNP this should benefit all residents, even if only after a few years. The exception to this would be introduction of the nativist policies identified by Piketty, as a response.

But what of the immigrants – what impacts do they have? Enrico Moretti tells us that "America's innovation hubs are a magnet for hardworking foreign-born entrepreneurs and scientists". Immigrants are more likely to have an advanced university degree than are the native born. He refers to a map published by Brookings that shows the cities in which immigrants have higher levels of education than do the native born. Furthermore, a one percent increase in the number of immigrant university graduates increases patents per capita by between 9 and 18 percent. Immigrant held patents tend to be computer technology and pharmaceuticals, while native born patent holders tend to be in traditional manufacturing areas. Forty-four metropolitan areas host highly skilled migrants, while 30 attract those who are lower educated. (Moretti, pp. 236–40) While the former tend to be centers of learning, of technology and of research, the latter are often cities with beef, pork or poultry processing plants, or places like Amazon distribution centers, in which lower-skilled, or unskilled, usually immigrant labor is employed.

To a significant degree the immigrant and native-born workers inhabit separate work spaces. Only the lowest skilled natives are in competition with migrants for rather undesirable jobs. These natives, of course, are the backbone of the nativist and white-supremacist reaction to immigration. They do have a loss in quality of life, but it is hardly the fault of the immigrants – some education would have protected them. The rest of US residents will gain in quality of life as a result of the impact of having immigrants work their way through society.

AGE DISTRIBUTION

The age distribution of any population can be represented by a population pyramid, as depicted in Figure 5.1. Ages range from birth at the bottom of the figure to age 100 at the top. The percentage of the population at each of the 10-year levels from bottom to top in Figure 5.1 will not be the same, but will differ because of events such as a world war or a pandemic, or a reduction in the birth rate due to parental preference or an event such as the Great Depression of the 1930s, or natural lifecycle. The reduced births during the depression would make the bottom of the pyramid narrower than it is in the figure; the post-World War II baby boom would make it wider. Over time, the two distortions would move up through the pyramid. If one "Googles" population pyramid, one can find dynamic representations of the population's age distribution as it varies over the years. We will take up the issues related to an aging of the population in the next section, but for now we will confine our discussion simply to the issues that relate to the distribution of the population by age groups.

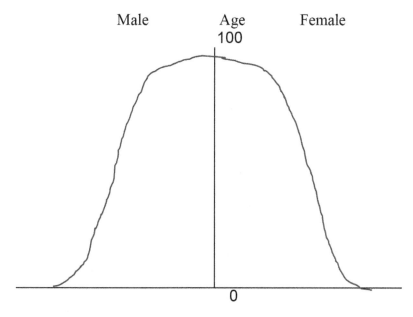

Figure 5.1   The optimal age distribution of the population

We can make some sense of this if we characterize each of the age groupings. For example, up to age 15 one is not really independent enough to differentiate oneself from those of other ages, but the 15–25 group can. This is an age of "becoming", one graduates from high school, and then a technical program, or a junior college, or a university or college. One then puts oneself on a path that will have a powerful impact on the rest of one's life. This is dramatically true for this age group today, in the age of the pandemic. High schools were without graduation ceremonies. Other groups with training or education may graduate this year, but even if they do not the quality of their education, obtained through distance learning, will not be of the caliber that they had expected. All of these groups have entered a work force that has been decimated by the virus. Thousands of shops, factories and service sector companies have either halted hiring, and have even been forced to let good and loyal employees join the ranks of the unemployed. Studies have shown that when young people have had experiences similar to this their lifetime earnings and status within a company have suffered. These consequences are often never overcome. Emma Dorn, Bryan Hancock, Jimmy Sarakatsannis and Ellen Viruleg have estimated, for McKinsey & Company, that the current K-12 student could lose lifetime earnings of $61,000 to $82,000. The longer in-class instruction is in abeyance, until Fall 2020 or January 2021 or Fall 2021, the number of high school dropouts is projected to increase by 232 or 648 or 1,100 students. (Dorn, et al.) Ippei Shibata demonstrated that the decline in employment for this cohort was twice as great in 2019–20 than for any other age group, and the employment loss diminished as workers were older. This impact was dramatically worse than it was in the Global Financial Crisis of 2007–08. (Shibata, pp. 10–11) These young people, both K-12 and those aged 15–25 years will be put on a dramatically less satisfying life path, and a less satisfying path with regard to both job satisfaction and quality of life. Normally this would be a positive quality of one's life, but the pandemic generation will, for the most, not have this experience.

Adults in their 30s, 40s, 50s, and 60s are in the prime period of life. This is when they form their families or other relationships, and experience what they will from their working life. This should be a high quality of life period for most of them, but of course divorce, unemployment, illness, loss of loved ones, and other disappointments intervene in the lives of many. And, of course, it is in this time of life that Case and Deaton's deaths of despair (see Chapter 1) exact their toll. So for this group little can be said in a general way. The probability of a high quality of life is there, but sadly not all are able to achieve this. The current pandemic will, of course, exacerbate the situation for those whose working lives are disrupted, and this may throw many adults off the track for decades, for others loved ones will suffer extended illness or even death, and many may never get back on track, so to speak. The possibilities here are too varied and unpredictable for us to write anything at all in a general sense.

The final group is those who are retired. This period is perhaps mindlessly referred to as the Golden Years, but this is true only for those who have been able to set aside sufficient funds to finance a satisfying retirement, and have the good health that will enable one to enjoy what is possible. During the period 1950–2020, US life expectancy of all residents increased from about 68 years to 79 years. At the beginning of the period, almost half of US residents did not live long enough to retire or to receive social security benefits. Today, he/she lives, on average, about 14 years beyond retirement age, in part because of better and more accessible healthcare and in part due to better lifestyles – primarily reduced use of tobacco. For most of the retired population quality of life probably is better than it was at earlier stages of life, but for many others retirement income is not adequate to support a satisfying life and access to healthcare may be lacking. While not suffering from "Deaths of Despair" they may live "lives of quiet desperation".

David Clark and William Hunter found, not surprisingly, that individuals in their working years are most attracted to a city by its labor market opportunities, and that "the impact of amenities on migration also follows a life-cycle pattern. Amenities are consistently found to influence middle-aged and older" individuals. And that "policy makers may be able to at least partially offset the deterrent effect of a poor mix of climatic amenities through the development of cultural and recreational amenities". (Clark and Hunter, p. 363) This supports what was argued here.

The short conclusion about age and quality of life, is that there is no uniform experience for groups of any age. The human condition is too varied and unpredictable to make any overall determination, especially in these pandemic years.

AGING

A separate but important issue is that of the economic consequences for a city of the aging of its population. I will be somewhat brief here as I have written extensively about this topic elsewhere. (Kresl and Ietri) At issue is the net benefit to a city of having a population that is increasingly composed of retired people, and, given their relationship to the city, the quality of life of those individuals. The tension is between the costs of having a population of retirees and the benefits gained from their presence. Figure 5.2 represents both costs and benefits to society of individuals as they go through their life. From birth to entry into the workforce there is a significant net cost to society, although considerable benefits accrue to the parents, of course.

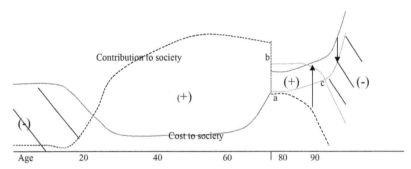

Note: The area "abc" is the potential gain to an urban economy from an aging population. Dotted line above the dashed line indicates a net cost to society. Dashed line above the dotted line indicates a net contribution to society.
Source: Peter Karl Kresl and Daniele Ietri, p. 70.

Figure 5.2   Lifelong net contribution to society

Then from age 20-something through retirement at about age 65 the cost to society, the dotted line, diminishes and the contribution to society, the dashed line, increased substantially. This net benefit continues until roughly age 65 at which age the contribution plummets and diminishes thereafter until death, while the cost to society makes a major and growing increase at that age. So that from age 65 on, there is a net and growing cost to society from having retirees in the population.

The costs to society of retirees are easily detailed. Retirees are dependent upon social programs to a greater degree than others except children. They require more access to healthcare than do others, long-term care is expensive, perhaps assistance in maintaining a household, and so forth. The benefits tend to diminish as they, generally, do not participate in the workforce and may be less engaged in social institutions. However, this is not the complete picture, for which we must consider what retirees do with their time. First, many engage in educational activities such as Lifelong Learning programs at universities and colleges throughout the country. Second, many of them engage in poetry, or novel, or public affairs reading groups. Third, audiences for opera, classical music, dance, and theater have always been dominated by seniors – this can be seen in films from the 1930s in which the audience for a musical event is shown, and from data that indicate that contemporary audiences are up to 75 or 80 percent aged 65 and older. As an aside, this should also add to the competitiveness of the city in relation to that of others. Fifth, retirees are often very active in participating in social or community or political organizations. The result of this intellectual engagement in a variety of community activities means that today's seniors are more likely to be active and independent in retirement and to be less reliant on social services for day-to-day living. This is represented in Figure 5.2 by the gray lines indicating an increase in the benefit and a reduction in the cost of the presence of a population of retirees.

Furthermore, during working years one tends to accumulate a retirement fund by not spending all of one's income. However, in retirement one does not save, one spends. So retirees tend to spend almost all of their income and this stimulates aggregate demand in the economy. In this case, the post-retirement experience for a society of a population of seniors should shift from the original net cost (the excess of the dotted over the dashed line) to a net benefit (the difference between the two gray lines). This should generate a shift toward an increase in the quality of life for the society as a whole and for the retirees as well.

POPULATION GROWTH RATE

People tend not to swim to a sinking ship, so if a city has an expanding population we can assume that those moving to it have an enhanced quality of life as a consequence of the move, although, depending upon their circumstances, objectively it may still be a rather low quality of life. Some migrants to the city may, of course, be disappointed. However, the primary issue is the impact of a growing city on the residents who are there before and during the growth period. At some point, the issue of the duration of the growth period will also become an issue for discussion.

During this year's pandemic many things about social services and social policy have become clearer than they have been. One of the primary ones is the fact that not all population growth change is voluntary and can be assumed to result in a better quality of life for the mover. Many people who have lost their jobs and have run through the various social programs find themselves without sufficient income to maintain the place of residence they had prior to the crisis. Many are, then, forced to give up their place of domicile and seek out another. If the second were preferable to the first we can assume that the individual or family would have already made this move. In this case, the change in population of the community will generate a loss in quality of life for the mover.

Increasing the number of people who live in a community has several rather obvious impacts on the quality of life of the original set of residents. More people means more support for retail outlets, up to a certain population a greater variety in the sorts of specialty shops, a greater variety of skills and knowledge in the population, a wider variety of companies that will find the community a viable place to establish a facility, more attendees at cultural institutions and festivals, and new people bringing new ideas. Population growth brings optimism to the community. These are true if the population grows from 20,000 to 25,000 or from 2 million to 2.5 million.

However, for the original residents the influx of new residents will generally mean that housing costs, for rentals as well as for home purchases, will rise. For homeowners this is a plus, but for renters they experience a loss in quality of life. Either they have less money for things other than rent or they have to move to another place. Again, this assumes that they had examined the alternatives for housing and were situated in the one that best met their needs, so any change could be assumed to involve a loss in quality of life.

POPULATION SIZE

We will examine the notion of an optimal city size in the next chapter. For now we can look at the consequences for the population of an ever larger collection of residents. We have just argued that a growing population can bring both benefits and costs to residents. But what is "too big", and how can this be determined? If one lives in a city of 15 or 20 million inhabitants, is this too big? Is a city of 25,000–50,000 too small? And what does this mean in terms of one's daily life? The danger is that one becomes isolated from others as the city enlarges and becomes less personalized. Unless one goes to church or joins a golf or tennis club, establishing relationships with others can be difficult. However, Jane Jacobs famously discussed the value and congeniality of the neighborhood, of which there are three types: (1) the whole city – all 20 million inhabitants, (2) the city district of about 100,000 inhabitants, and (3) street neighborhoods of perhaps a few hundred people. The latter is the solution to the impersonality of the first two. (Jacobs, p. 117) If one lives in a cohesive and sustaining street neighborhood one has little awareness of the rest of the 15 or 20 million others. So whether the city is 1 million or 20 million there is little impact on the resident of the street neighborhood, except in relation to things such as access to a major international airport. However, not all of us can live in a functioning street neighborhood. In fact, Jacob's beloved Hudson street neighborhood, with its open windows and people sitting on the steps so they can observe and protect local children, has been converted to buildings with sealed plate glass windows and with security systems that make it difficult for people to sit on the steps, so as to provide a security of a different kind.

Over time, of course, one becomes accustomed to the latest stage in the development of new forms of social settings, we cease to miss what we used to have and then we forget that we had it and acclimate ourselves to the new urban social environment. For those who experienced both versions of Hudson Street there would certainly be a loss of quality of life, but for the inhabitants of the "sealed" new units there would be no such loss. It may not be that the new residents do or don't experience greater or lesser quality of life from their neighborhood, but that they do not expect to get this from the place they happen to live, perhaps for a few years.

Indeed in many cities housing in developments on the city edges is of the cookie cutter variety, *à la* Malvina Reynolds, so they can be sold quickly in a labor force that tends to move every three to five years for career advancement. Not much neighborhood here, and perhaps not much sought.

The three remaining issues, religion, race and sexual identification, have become hot-button items in our political discourse and in our lives as citizens of the US. We have discussed the issue of tolerance in Chapter 2 and found it to be an essential element in any city that seeks to be competitive in the contemporary economy. Each will be discussed individually here.

RELIGION

Religion will be treated first, and, to some degree, separately since while one's race or sexual identification are essentially not a preference, one's religion is. While we may be born into a family of a specific religious belief and may spend our first years or decades living in that faith, we always have the option to leave it for one that offers something more congenial or satisfying. Religions differ with regard to their demands on our time and being, their comprehensiveness, their isolation from other faiths and non-believers, and the rigidity of their doctrine. Hence, it is very easy for members of one faith to perceive those of other faiths as being of lesser value or too permissive or too confining and this can easily lead to disdain, conflict, and an urge to proselytize. These sentiments all lead to intolerance and conflict and even to war. They certainly do nothing for a society's competitiveness in the world economy.

The Mormons, or LDS, are a case in point. They have a very cohesive and closed faith and seek to proselytize to gain new believers in all parts of the world. Their base is in Salt Lake City, and the primary LDS university of Brigham Young University. As they have sought to capture some of the benefits of the larger society they have had to make some accommodations to the rest of the world. Elements in their belief and practice included polygamy, and opposition to the Equal Rights Amendment, gambling, consumption of alcohol, and same sex marriage. In recent years the church has accommodated its beliefs and these and other practices to be more acceptable to the outer world. This is largely due to the desire to develop Salt Lake City and other cities in Utah as technologically sophisticated and more effectively tolerant counterparts to Seattle, Silicon Valley, Austin, Boston and other cities of the high tech world. These accommodations have made Utah, with its outdoor assets – skiing, hiking, fishing, hunting, etc. – more attractive to a technologically sophisticated labor force. In this effort they have been quite successful.

The city and quality of life

Table 5.1   *US racial composition 1970, 1990, and 2010*

	1970	1990	2010	2010–1970
White	87.7	80.3	72.4	−15.3
Black	11.1	12.1	12.6	1.5
Native	0.4	0.8	0.9	0.5
Asian	0.8	2.9	4.9	4.1
Other	0.1	3.9	6.2	6.1
Hispanic	4.4	9.0	16.3	11.9
Non-Hispanic White	83.5	75.6	63.7	−19.8

Source: US Census Bureau, via Wikipedia.org

Catholics, evangelicals and Southern Baptists have all had to make accommodations to a more secular workforce if they are to be successful in the broader world. The development of cities in the South, such as Atlanta, Athens, Raleigh, Greensboro, Tuscaloosa, Oxford, and Tallahassee, among others, are all examples of this necessity to be tolerant to non-believers. Those religious communities that remain closed, suspicious of those of other faiths, or no faith, have difficulty in emerging into the modern tech-dominated world economy. Presumably, these individuals experience a high level of quality of life. In a step similar to that of the LDS, Southern Baptists have just voted to remove "Southern" from their name, so as to more clearly cut the tie to the church's slavery-dominated past.

RACIAL COMPOSITION AND TENSION

Race continues to be the most divisive and confrontational issue of social policy in the US, as well as in many other parts of the world. In the US the racial composition has gradually changed especially since 1970. Table 5.1 gives the percentage for the major groups for 1970, 1990, and 2010. The salient point of this history is the rather dramatic decline in the percentage of the population that is non-Hispanic white. The primary increase was in the Hispanic population, with Blacks virtually unchanged and with Asians having a small gain. The projection for 2050 is that the non-Hispanic white population will fall a further 16.7 percentage points to 47 percent, Hispanics will rise to 29 percent, Asians will rise to 9 percent and Blacks will be unchanged.

The dominant political issue today is the decline in the non-Hispanic white population from a dominant position in 1990 to a minority by 2050. This causes extreme angst among non-Hispanic whites, especially for those lacking in education and skills, and generates much of the basis for the white-supremacist and similar movements that have become so prominent in our political life today. The Trump administration has based much of its struggle for popularity on the prospect of the US becoming majority non-white society and the threat this poses for this component of the population, and of the electorate.

Earlier, in Chapter 3, we discussed the negative impact that racial intolerance has on urban competitiveness. This has certainly had its impact on the economies of many US cities; however, in many others racial intolerance has not spilled over into the white dominated economy due to residential segregation which has formed a barrier around the Black districts of the city. In Chicago, the major Black neighborhoods have been on the South Side of the central business district, centered on The Loop, defined by an elevated transit line. As Blacks sought to move northward and encroach on The Loop and the major central shopping district the city sought to place barriers in their path. First the campus of the University of Illinois at Chicago and then closer to The Loop The Harold Washington Public Library situated like a cork at the northern end, the bottle's neck, of State Street, the main route to and from the South Side.

There are several other costs to society of racial discrimination. If we start close to the beginning, there are several gains to society from racially integrating our schools, from the first years on. In integrated schools low-income students (many of whom are other than Asian or non-Hispanic white) have higher than average test scores, they are more likely to enroll in college, they are less likely to drop out, and they are more engaged in critical thinking, problem solving, and creativity. Furthermore they are likely to seek out integrated settings, they have more intellectual self-confidence, and as adults they will have higher earnings, improved health, and lower rates of incarceration. (The Century Foundation) Racial segregation negates all of these gains. It is also the case that in racially segregated work environments, Black workers advance to a point in the corporate structure but then stagnate because they have no Black mentors to guide them through the corporate structure. Black women are especially impacted by this. They earn 89 percent of what a Black man earns, and he earns 74 percent of a white man, hence, a Black woman earns 65 percent of a white man. "Black families face systemic, intersecting barriers that limit their wealth building. Left unchecked, these gaps could continue to grow and constrain the US economy, not just black families". (Noel, et al., pp. 14–19) This leads to a lowering of the quality of life of all US residents, not just Blacks.

It is a curious feature of the current pandemic and the reaction of cities public to it, that those who are protesting and parading against racial discrimination bring forth a violent response from the armed white-separatists and similar groups which may indeed generate publicity and a diminution of the competitiveness of cities such as Portland, Oregon, and Kenosha, Wisconsin, to name just the two most prominent cities. It is hard to see how the racial dis-

crimination and the protesting that is a response to it is enhancing the quality
of life of anyone, except for some who thrive on this sort of turmoil, unless
the turmoil enhances the political strength of the movement that is supported
by this.

President Trump has rather famously insulted or tried to bar entry to
a variety of foreign-born migrants. Muslims, Mexicans, Central Americans,
Africans, Chinese, and just about everyone but northern Europeans such
as Norwegians, although a country filled with Social Democrats who have
a strong appreciation of and regard for government would not help to create
the society he seeks to introduce. This would diminish the quality of life of the
President and all of his supporters.

SEXUAL IDENTIFICATION

Discrimination against individuals who identify as other than simply male or
female has been a feature of most societies for centuries. In the US, individuals escaped discrimination and harassment by hiding their true preference or
identity. This has been the subject of many works of literature and of film for
many years, but in the last couple of decades there has been a movement of
self-identification, coming out, that has begun to force the situation to evolve
dramatically. Well-known individuals have announced their true sexuality and
in most cases no longer suffer ostracism or disadvantage in the workplace or
in other places in society. Some individuals do, however, continue to ostracize
and to discriminate against LGBTQ and others who declare a "non-standard"
sexuality. Clearly, this declaration has increased the quality of life of those
who have had to hide their true identity for fear of disadvantage in work and
in social life, and probably diminished it for those who are distressed by this
openness. Not many people would now give much weight to the discomfort of
the latter.

Economists have long argued that a firm or a society that discriminates, on
the basis of race, or religion, or ethnicity, or sexual preference, or whatever, will
be less efficient and competitive in relation to those who do not discriminate.
(Marshall) Hiring a less competent "good old boy" rather than a competent
LGBT individual will negatively affect the efficiency, the quality and the price
of what is being produced. This is one of the reasons for the inferior economic
status of the American South until recent years, when this discrimination had
to be scrapped. An economy that does not discriminate will function more
competitively and with less overt conflict than one that does, and this point is
being made continually today and cities are introducing policies and norms to
ensure this will be the case. The cost of continuing to discriminate is simply
too high, in addition to the morality of doing this. Ultimately, the quality of
life of almost all residents will be enhanced by non-discrimination. However,

it remains the case that in some situations individuals will be denied access to institutions of learning that will lower educational and skill attainment of those who are the result of these barriers to access by race or sexual identification. Thus the less than satisfying situation of some of these individuals may not be based solely on their racial or sexual identity but on other factors of discrimination that will have an impact on their productivity.

Nonetheless, the cost to society of discrimination on the basis of sexual identification is real and substantial, as it is with all forms of discrimination.

FINAL THOUGHTS

Demography has the potential to cause great conflict and tension within a city's residents. Even without conflict it is one of the most important areas of the aspects of a city and of its public policy; it can, and does, have significant impacts on the quality of life of residents. Some of the most contentious issues, such as discrimination against any of several categories of the population, have powerful impacts, not just due to the impacts of these actions on individuals but also because of the negative impact they can have on the city's competitiveness, as noted in Chapter 3. There are also further negative impacts on the efficiency of the operation of the city's economy and on the incomes that can be generated from the city's assets and productive resources, and this should have a negative impact on the quality of life of all residents.

Migration, which can be, and usually is, a positive event for a society, has been turned by demagoguery, ignorance and irrational fear into a powerful and divisive political issue. When societies, such as most of the Western democracies, Russia, China, and many others, have aging populations and declining rates of natality, the resultant shrinking of the population calls the future sustainability of the national economies into question. Advances in technology and innovations in the nature and structure of work can help in maintaining aggregate output, and income, but the actual realization of this is not at all assured. Migration has been historically the best policy option for improving the population pyramid. It is often the case that the increase in the quality of life of the migrants is not taken into account in the determination of the benefits to the receiving society.

Migration has a powerful impact on the age distribution of the population, but also on the productivity of the economy of the city through the work ethic of immigrants and their stimulation of creativity and entrepreneurship. On the other hand, by increasing the city population they do put pressure on the availability of housing, and the cost of rent and home ownership. But issues of the availability of housing both for minorities and for the population as a whole have been with us for decades and the influx of immigrants has not exacerbated this situation in most cities.

We have just discussed at length the consequences for a city and its population of discrimination with regard to race, religion and sexual preference. Needless to say, there are no positive consequences of this, certainly not for the quality of life for city residents. These issues could be treated rather easily with public policy, but segments of the population and of the Congress and the political system in general are intransigent in their resistance to change for, what must be called objectively, the better, and only powerful forces in the society will be able to effect change. During 2020, and the years leading up to it, a series of horrific events have taken place to the effect that opposition to discrimination and anti-immigration sentiment has grown, among both minority and white populations. Given our history it is never wise to be too optimistic for improvement, but the sentiment at this time does give one reason to hope for resolution of some long-standing social beliefs and practices. Progress in these areas could bring a genuine improvement in the quality of life of the vast majority of residents in our cities and of the nation as a whole.

REFERENCES

Clark, David E. and William J. Hunter, "The Impact of Economic Opportunity, Amenities and Fiscal Factors on Age-specific Migration rates", *Journal of Regional Science*, Vol. 32, No. 3, 1992, pp. 349–65.

Dorn, Emma, Bryan Hancock, Jimmy Sarakatsannis and Ellen Viruleg, "COVID-19 and student learning in the United States: The hurt could last a lifetime", in Joshua G. Freeman, *Behemoth: A History of the Factory and the Making of the Modern World*, New York, W. W. Norton, 2018.

Glaeser, Edward L., *The Economic Approach to Cities*, NBER Working Paper 13696, Cambridge: National Bureau of Economic Research, December 2007.

Jacobs, Jane, *The Death and Life of Great American Cities*, New York: Vintage Books, 1992.

Kresl, Peter Karl and Daniele Ietri, *The Aging Population and the Competitiveness of Cities, Benefits to the Urban Economy*, Cheltenham, UK and Northampton, MA, USA: Edward Elgar, 2010.

McKinsey and Company, 1 June 2020.

Marshall, Ray, "The Economics of Racial Discrimination: A Survey", *Journal of Economic Literature*, Vol. 12, No. 3, September 1974, pp. 849–71.

Milanovic, Branko, *Global Inequality, A New Approach for the Age of Globalization*, Cambridge: The Belknap Press of Harvard University Press, 2016.

Moretti, Enrico, *The New Geography of Jobs*, New York: Houghton Mifflin Harcourt, Boston: 2012.

Noel, Nick, Duwain Pinder, Shelley Steward III and Jason Wright, *The Economic Impact of Closing the Racial Wealth Gap*, Washington: McKinsey and Company, 2019.

Piketty, Thomas, *Capital in the Twenty-first Century*, Cambridge: The Belknap Press of Harvard University Press, 2014.

Shibata, Ippei, *The Distributional Impact of Recession: The Global Financial Crisis and the Pandemic Recession*, Washington: International Monetary Fund, 20 June 2010.

6. Urban attributes and quality of life

A city's attributes are its characteristic qualities. Essentially, they are the things that define the city. On the one hand, they are what makes the city different from other cities; while on the other hand they are the qualities that endear the city to its residents, or that make them dissatisfied with it. Some attributes are physical things or spaces that have been created by the city's planners and residents; residents enjoy using them or spending time with them. They can also be things that they see on a regular basis – the beauty of a well-designed park or of a building or other structure. They need not enter any of these constructs to enjoy them. Residents usually have an understanding of just how the attributes of the city in which they live differ from those of some other cities, so their appreciation is an informed one and not simply an irrational attachment.

In this chapter we can examine seven attributes that have an impact on the quality of life of the city's residents: (1) civic pride, (2) renown or image, (3) architecture, (4) imaginative spaces, that is, parks and waterfronts, (5) optimal size, (6) isolation or connectedness, and (7) effective government. In Chapter 5, we saw that there was much contention and strife among some of the aspects of demographics, and almost every one of them was the cause of considerable tension within individual elements of the population. Hence, it was not possible to find a generally positive impact on quality of life for these aspects. We will not find such tension between city attributes and elements of the residential population. Now we will turn to examination of each of the attributes.

CIVIC PRIDE

Developing pride in one's home town is instrumental in strengthening a shared community identity, active citizenship, collective memory, social cohesion, and a sense of community ownership. It is "part of what defines and shapes cities, and forms an important lens through which they are imagined and governed". (Collins, p. 175) Cynthia Nikitin goes so far as to say: "Civic institutions, such as parks, libraries, city halls and cultural facilities, are the foundations of a civil society and the cornerstones of democracy". Taking pride in them has "the potential to once again anchor communities, bringing them together both physically and symbolically by providing resources, gathering places and forums for open communication". She refers back a century ago to the local courthouses that were constructed in central places with retail, public markets, places to eat and to drink and that supported and indeed created the civic pride of the day. Sadly, she says, "the idea of civic engagement taking place in and around institution has fallen out of favor for a number of reasons ... includ(ing) bureaucracy, safety and security concerns". (Nikitin, p. 10) Now we have to create other institutions and places to replace the courthouse squares that fostered civic price and community.

The arts are often proposed as a vehicle for furthering a sense of civic pride. As Ruth Rentschler, Kerrie Bridson and Jody Evans wrote: "Civic pride and community identity occur at both the collective community and individual levels through successful execution of cultural policy that facilitates and promotes identity formation". They are Australians and speak of a culture that includes Indigenous, European and Asian populations. So building a sense of community is a significant challenge. Participation of all groups in a collective arts and culture community helps to provide a space for Indigenous representation as well as creating a sense of Australian uniqueness and of a shared collective sense of identity.

Two smaller towns that have pursued the arts as a way of defining the community and of building a sense of local pride are Chemainus, on Victoria Island in British Columbia, and San Angelo, Texas. Each has supported local artists in giving representations of the local community, its history and its collective identity. Chemainus has 44 murals and 10 sculptures – all from a town of 3,035 inhabitants. San Angelo has a population of 88,000 and 14 murals. In both cities the murals, depicting local scenes and historical events and persons, are on the sides of buildings so they can be seen and studied by all who pass them. These are two examples of how art can help to create a unique city vision. They also help in marketing the town to tourists and investors. It is the case that many inner-city neighborhoods have used wall paintings and other works of art to "transform a negative image of their neighborhood into a positive one". We see this almost weekly on our television. (Creative City Network of Canada, p. 3)

Suggesting the downside of civic pride is a study done by Rachel Kranton, Seth Sanders and Matthew Pease in which they studied group membership and discrimination. They examined 141 individuals and concluded that when one desires to be part of a group, then that person is more likely to discriminate against non-members. We are all unavoidably members of groups, our sex, race, nationality, and so forth, and some of us discriminate against others who are members of other groups. What is more nefarious is when we choose to join, for example, a political party or faction. Having chosen this we tend to want to make our loyalty to it explicit. We can do this by banding together against another political group. This is descriptive of US political culture of today, of course, and it can, and has, led to violence. One thinks of religious and territorial conflict and war in our history. Civic pride rarely takes this form and can be useful if it leads a civic population to strive to outdo another. Such healthy competition can lead all participants to perform better and to generate a gain in quality of life for all. At least, this is the hope.

Before leaving the subject of civic pride, we should take note of the consequence of failure to do the things discussed above. William Polito wrote about Altoona, Pennsylvania, for his local newspaper. The title of his piece says it all – "Pride lacking in city residents". In something of a take-off on the "Broken Windows" approach of James Q. Wilson and George L. Kelling, Polito notes junk cars, piles of trash, uncut grass, and houses that need a coat of paint. Once this starts, it has a life of its own. "If people want to live like that on the inside of their house, that's fine but on the outside, it represents safety hazards, sanitation issues, breeds pests and drastically impacts property values". It is not a question of money – what does a trash bag cost? The city has codes but lacks enforcement. "The city is an absolute mess and getting worse all the time. Does anyone care?" (Polito)

RENOWN OR IMAGE

A city's image is a complex creation that combines both past accomplishments and past failures, it has to be embedded in the current reality of the economy and society, and it has to speak to the aspirations and hopes of the residents. This set of elements is very likely to contain contradictions and residents have to forge out of this a consistent story of the city and a coherent vision of its future. Some images are the result of a well-conceived campaign to project a combination of aspirations and reality, while others are out of the control of the residents and leaders of the city. Pittsburgh is a city with an image from the past that, on the one hand, connects current residents with the city of their parents and grandparents through visions of a city that was so darkened with industrial smoke from steel mills that it was sometimes difficult to see more than 100 yards, but it was also a city of hard work, muscle, unions, labor conflicts, and production of a product that supported the entire US economy. Today that image has been altered to encompass an economy of medical technology, and of robots and information technology. Pittsburghers have pride when they look back into history or forward into the era of the high tech economy. The image of the city is positive and functional.

Almost every city has either been labeled by others or developed its own image. Examples are numerous and obvious: Paris the City of Light, Chicago The Windy City, New York the Big Apple, Philadelphia the city of Brotherly Love, San Francisco The City by the Bay, Denver the Mile High City, Rome the Eternal City, Gallup, New Mexico, Drunk Driving Capital of the World and Cape Hatteras, North Carolina, Graveyard of the Atlantic. Some cities are serious about this, while others do it with tongue in cheek. But all see the need to project an image of the city to the rest of the world. The image may be one of affirmation or of self-deprecation, but anything is better than being just another anonymous dot on a map.

There are many other cities that have this combination of backward and forward looking aspects of a city's image. Chicago, Seattle, and San Francisco are good examples of this. In all cases, the residents of the city look backward with a certain pride and anticipate a future that will be filled with accomplishment. The historically industrial cities, Detroit, Youngstown and Cleveland, and even St. Louis, can look back with a certain pride, but now see themselves being passed by Columbus and Pittsburgh. The causes are varied and include technological change, the rise of competition elsewhere in the US or in the world economy, racial conflict and "white flight", local corruption, and simple lack of attention from city leaders.

Specialists in this area tell us that creating an image can be very useful if it "includes the place's vision, the involvement and motivation of all the place's internal and external customers and users and its economic, social and cultural consequences". (Ashworth and Kavaratzis, p. 238) Detroit gives us an example of how this can go wrong. Entrepreneurs such as Dan Gilbert, head of Quicken Loans, bought up cheap land and buildings in the deteriorated downtown and other districts making up 7.2 square miles of Detroit's 142 square miles, and invested heavily in it. Restored buildings, housing, retail, etc. – all the things a gentrifying city area needs. As for the remaining 134.8 square miles, there was little recovery. Peter Moskowitz notes that "gentrification is simply a new form of the same process that created the suburbs; it's the same age-old racist process of subsidizing and privileging the lives and preferred locales of the wealthy and white over those of poor people of color". (Moskowitz, p. 117) One of the early consultants to Detroit was Richard Florida. After several years of observing the situation in the city he was forced to conclude: "We need to be clear that ultimately, we can't stop the decline of some places, and that we would be foolish to try". (Moskowitz, p. 82) Apparently some cities simply are not amenable to transformation by means of development of the "creative class".

The capacity of the quality of life to be enhanced by development of renown or a positive image depends very much upon the relationship of the citizen to the economy of the city. The image creates positive value for those who are in the favored sector of the economy, but does little other than some minor spillover for those who are not. This is more generalized than just Detroit, as all cities have their specific problems with racial and other segregation and discrimination, income extremes, exclusion, lack of mobility, and so forth. A positive image has the capacity to carry along a segment of the city's population and to increase their quality of life, but for many others this does not happen, nor is it possible.

ARCHITECTURE

A city's architecture is its face to the world. The first time we see it we gain an understanding about the values, self-esteem, ambition, brashness, and aspirations, its past and its future, and the esthetics of that city. The Eiffel Tower told us toward the end of the 19th century that Paris, a city of culture and beauty, aspired to be a city of industry, modernity, and science. The Petronas Towers in Kuala Lumpur give an indication that the city is "in its flight to the future". The tallest building in the world in 1998 was designed by an international star, Cesar Pelli, who told us that Kuala Lumpur was announcing itself to the world. The Burj Khalifa in Dubai and the Kingdom Tower in Jeddah, assert the presence and economic status of United Arab Emirates and Saudi Arabia as modern and forward looking countries. In the US, the Sears (now Willis) Tower announced that Chicago, the birth city of the skyscraper, still valued first-class architecture, and the replacement of the World Trade Center, destroyed on 11 September 2001, by the One World Trade Center brashly declared that New York City was still in the game, so to speak. We learn so much about a city from its premier and principal architecture. The brashness and optimism of these architectural initiatives lift the spirits of the city's residents, give them a positive identity, and thereby enhance their quality of life.

Occasionally there is a clash of two competing visions of the city and its future. An example of this is in St. Louis when it decided to construct the Gateway Arch, symbolizing the gateway to the West. The arch was designed by Eero Sarinen and was intended to symbolize the city's look to the future – "the rebirth of St. Louis". Critic Ada Louise Huxtable found it to be a failure as an urban project. What was destroyed in the space of the Arc was a 40 square block area of the city's "priceless cast-iron architectural heritage" and what was created was "monument to Chamber of Commerce planning and design". Planned in this site were a stadium, parking garages, and access to superhighways, and in the process St. Louis "gained a lot of real estate and lost a historic city". (quoted in Campbell, pp. 162–3) There is often controversy over an architectural project, but the destruction of the cast-iron district ended up killing the area, as things planned for did not materialize and the commercial, retail and cultural activity abandoned the center of the city and it shifted to the western side of town. It would be a complex question as to what happened to the quality of life of St. Louis' residents as a consequence.

Fortunately, there are many other examples in which architectural projects enhanced quality of life and gave an identity to the city. Santa Fe is a prime example. At the beginning of the 20th century the city was threatened with being isolated when the Santa Fe railroad management decided to use a somewhat shorter route that would bypass the city and then again in the 1930s when a governor who lost an election blamed it on the opposition of Santa Fe merchants and re-routed US 66. The response to this potential decline was design of the "Santa Fe Style" or "Spanish Pueblo Revival Style" of architecture that replaced whole districts of bungalows and Victorian style houses. The structures of earth toned adobe, hewn wood beams, lintels, and corbels have come to make the city distinctive and recognizable. This architecture served to attract the tourists and others of whom Santa Fe had been deprived by transportation initiatives out of their control. The city has become very popular due to the architecture and a number of cultural institutions that have been built there, such as Museum Hill, the Georgia O'Keefe Museum, and the Santa Fe Opera, among others.

A final example of what architecture can do to vitalize a smaller town is given by Columbus, Indiana. Another Saarinen, this time Eliel, entered the picture in 1942 with a contract to build a modern Finnish style church for the city, by J. Irwin Miller, the head of the Cummins Engine Corporation. This led to establishment of the Cummins Engine Foundation, the sole mission of which was to pay the commissions of noted architects, on a list, to design municipal buildings and structures for the city. This has led to 70 buildings and structures, and 30 works of public art by architects such as Eliel and his son Eero, Robert Venturi, Cesar Pelli, Robert Stern, and I. M. Pei, and work by sculptors such as Henry Moore, Dale Chihuly, Robert Indiana and Jean Tinguely. The American Institute of Architects ranks Columbus behind only Chicago, New York San Francisco, Boston and Washington as centers of architecture – this for a town of about 40,000 inhabitants. Columbus is on the itinerary of all serious students of public architecture who visit the US. Clearly the quality of life of the residents of Columbus has been enhanced by this initiative of Mr. Miller and the Cummins Engine Foundation.

We have seen in this section how public architecture can have a transformative impact on a city, if done right. This does not always happen, of course, but either way an architectural project does have an impact on the quality of life of the residents who may encounter the structure(s) on a daily basis. For further discussion I refer the reader to a book I wrote with Daniele Ietri, *Creating Cities/Building Cities*. (Kresl and Ietri, 2017)

IMAGINATIVE SPACES – PARKS AND WATERFRONTS

While we are inspired from a distance by good architecture that looms over us, parks and waterfronts invite us to enter where we hope to find quiet, space for reflection and for restoration, and beauty. We can stroll through the formal, geometric French parks or enter the equally planned natural countryside of their English counterparts. Each is an allocation of land to non-productive, green space in the midst of a bustling city. While they are quite different in their philosophy, each invites us to abandon the often frenetic pace of the urban world for a time of quiet repose, reflection and beauty. Both French and English parks were largely on land that was transferred from royal to public ownership, whereas US parks are largely on land that was purchased and cleared for public use, with the exception of the country's first cities, such as Savannah, Philadelphia and Boston, in which parks were included in the original plan of the city space. This says nothing about National Parks which are far from urban centers and have different rationales and impact, which will not be discussed here.

City parks serve residents and different constituencies in several important ways. Some are substantial such as the positive impact that development of a park has on the market value of the adjacent properties. This has been noted as a virtually universal phenomenon from Central Park in Manhattan to Regent's Park in London to Yorkville Park in Toronto. They also tend to lower crime rates and enhance levels of perceived safety (Tate, pp. 194 and 198) Parks enable residents to find places to meet and to play, and to stroll and do other activities that enhance their healthiness. For Frederick Law Olmstead, parks were places for residents to escape the oppressive conditions of the city. His partner, Calvert Vaux, thought that a city would evolve by means of democratic use by residents and that it would evolve in accordance with their demands and use, not simply in accordance with the ideas of the planners. (Tate, p. 150) One of the most ambitious park initiatives was Daniel Burnham's Plan for Chicago in 1906. While not fully implemented it did accomplish a set of parks along Lake Michigan that extended seven miles north and eight miles south from Grant Park and gave every resident of Chicago streetcar ride access to the parks, the lake and the beaches.

A contrast to Chicago is given by Detroit, a city which has never developed access to its water front, consisting of Lake Detroit and the St. Clair River. Access by residents to the metropolitan area has been blocked by the Grosse Pointes, the Park, the Farms, the Shores, and Woods. Nothing done by GMs Renaissance Center or by Dan Gilbert developing the 7.2 square miles in the downtown area did anything to give residents access to the water. Other cities have made impressive efforts during the past three decades to develop waterfronts that had been abandoned by previously viable shipping companies but had moved to more efficient areas nearby. New York has developed Battery Park and the Southport Museum areas, as well as the extensive Riverside Park on the Upper West Side. Boston has converted its dock area to Faneuil Hall area and a set of museums on the waterfront. Equally impressive has been Baltimore's resurrection of its Inner Harbor area with retail, restaurants and hotels, as well as a very successful National Aquarium.

One final set of examples we could examine are the elevated parkways and walkways that have been constructed on what had long been functioning center city railways. The first was the Promenade Plantée in Paris that utilized an elevated rail line from the train station at Bastille to that at Vincennes. In 1993, the elevated "trail" was converted into a walkway with plantings, and with several access points along it. At ground level there is a series of 71 viaducts, many of which have been converted to retail shops, restaurants, galleries, and 45 craft workshops. It has been extremely successful. Six years later, Mayor Giuliani in New York wanted to demolish an elevated rail line in Lower West Side Manhattan. Before he could do this, he was replaced by Michael Bloomberg, who saw the potential and halted the destruction and initiated planning of the High Line. After several years of construction, the High Line was opened in three sections in 2009, 2011 and 2014. It has become as popular as its predecessor in Paris. Paul Goldberger wrote that the old line had become a "remnant of a different kind of city (that) had to be removed for the neighborhood to realize its full potential". (Goldberger, 2011) Perhaps the same could have been said of the former mayor, as well! Other cities, such as Chicago with its "606", have undertaken to do similar projects.

As a final comment, I refer to the work of Anne Power, Jörg Plöger and Astrid Winkler in their book *Phoenix Cities*. After examining the decline and recovery of seven cities in Europe, they conclude that in each case: "City councils determined that rebuilding a 'sense of place' was a prerequisite for recovery. They could only achieve this by reinvesting in central squares, civic monuments and existing urban neighborhoods". (Power, et al., p. 33)

There are many other city parks and waterfronts we could examine but I think the examples given here are sufficient to make the point. That point being that both city parks and restored waterfronts can have powerfully positive impacts on the quality of life of city residents.

OPTIMAL SIZE

In Chapter 4 we examined the consequences of a city that is growing and one that is contracting, primarily on the availability and cost of housing, but also the creation and destruction of aspects of city districts such as retail, social spaces such as bars and restaurants, and the consequences for elements of the population of gentrification. Here we are, so to speak, taking a still shot of a city and the consequences of its being larger rather than smaller. This raises the question as to whether there is an optimal size for a city. Economists have given a wide variety of answers to this question. Economists considering city size analyze the effects of economies of agglomeration, economies of scale, effects of diversity, availability of public and other services, the crime rate, environmental effects and sustainability, among other things. But there is little agreement as regards optimal city size. An OECD study suggested that, for productivity reasons, about 6 million residents would be optimal. Boris Begovic thought that 500,000 would be a bit too large, and Roberto Camagni, Roberta Capello and Andrea Caragliu settled on 714,973 as the optimal size for a city. (OED 2006, ch. 1; Begovic, 1991; Camagni, Capello and Caragliu, 2015, p. 1083) No one suggests that the world's largest cities, with 20 million or more residents are in any way optimal.

A larger population could have a negative impact on quality of life of those involved, but when looking at the time given to commuting, researchers find that no matter how large the city the time devoted to commuting remains almost constant. (Jaffee) One-way commutes were 21.7 minutes in 1980 and 25.3 in 2010, and from 2000 and 2010 they declined from 25.5 minutes to 25.3. When individuals move to a city they can seek to avoid a decline in quality of life as population size differs, by either: (1) changing from a personal car to public transportation, (2) moving to a location that is closer to work, or (3) taking a job that is closer to the home they have purchased. The crucial point here is that local government must provide suitable alternative ways to commute.

With regard to creativity in cities of different sizes, Richard Florida has tended to focus on larger cities, but Charles Landry stated that "every city can be more creative than it currently is and the task for a city wanting to be creative is to identify, nurture, harness, promote, attract and sustain talent and to mobilize ideas, resources and organizations ... Smaller cities can try out things a central city may find unimportant". (Landry, p. 412) Allen Scott wrote of "associated networks of small towns that participate in the new cognitive-cultural economy". He then discusses "the rising demands in large cities" for things that are produced in the smaller cities, and concludes: "while the new cognitive-cultural economy is predominantly concentrated in major cities, it is far from being confined to large urban areas, and is, in fact, making its presence increasingly felt in a diversity of interstitial spaces". What one finds in smaller cities is landscape, authenticity versus debasement, preservation versus modernization, the traditional store of know-how. (Scott, ch. 9) Not exactly Karl Marx's "idiocy of rural life", but then capitalism of today is far from that of the mid-19th century.

The smaller town or city characteristics just listed are not in themselves sufficient to make a smaller place vital and competitive, however, and Anne Lorentzen suggests that there are three conditions that should be considered to be vital: (1) affluence, (2) globalization, and (3) mobility/accessibility. Without affluence the smaller city will lack the luxury demands that are necessary for leisure, culture and the experience economy that seem to be necessary for economic success. Globalization integrates the smaller city into "the global flow of knowledge, information, people and money" that integrate it into the larger world of economic competitiveness. Finally, without mobility/accessibility neither of the other two conditions will be attainable. The smaller city cannot be successful if it is not integrated into the larger world.

The point here is to note that smaller cities can find their places in the world of large cities. Individuals can, then, choose among cities of all sizes when they decide to settle down for an indefinite period of time. This gives them the opportunity to create for themselves a living and working arrangement that will maximize their quality of life.

ISOLATION OR CONNECTEDNESS

By the end of the 20th century, being isolated or not connected was fatal for a city that sought to participate in the modern economy. Connection can be done either by local institutions and individuals participating on their own account or through organizations that enable them to share experiences and to gain from those of others.

While isolation and connectedness a few decades ago related to rail, air and telephone technology, today to be connected means being connected by telecommunications, both for individuals and for cities and companies. The pandemic has shown us how important this can be just to participate in contemporary society. School and university students are being forced to do distance learning from home. Sadly, many of these students do not have high-speed, or any, internet connection at home, and the household may not even own a computer. The consequence for these young people for the rest of their lives will be exclusion from many of the employment options that would otherwise have been open to them and for which they would be very suitable, substantially lower life-time earnings, shorter life span, life on the margin, and more probability of being subjected to poorer health and to deaths of despair. Hardly an increase in their quality of life. For most Americans, by the time they are 20 years old, the die has been cast for them. Chicagoans Barack Obama and Ken Griffin donated money for 100,000 Chrome Book computers to be given to low-income families in the city. This need exists in many other US cities.

This connectedness is crucial if young students are going to be able to function in the economy of today, let alone that of tomorrow. Obviously, students who grow up with computers at hand will be most capable of functioning effectively in the economy in which they will be living and working. The economy they will confront will not only require familiarity with a computer but also all of the things one can do with this technology. It will be required for the vast majority of employment possibilities they will encounter. Familiarity with all of these computer applications may very well be what separates those workers who thrive in the world of tomorrow from those who cannot quite manage it. Some workers will always find good employment in jobs in welding, metal work, design, and other eye, hand and muscle work but others will be left on the sidelines, as has always been the case. If the pandemic consequences force our society to confront some of these fundamental dividing lines we may be able to create places that will be satisfying to this group of young entrants to the workforce. If not, they may form the nucleus of a segment of our society that is continually distressed, alienated and potentially disruptive. This may become one of the major challenges to the rest of society.

Cities are connected to the world that is of importance to them through organizations such as The Conference of US Mayors and The National League of Cities, discussed in Chapter 4. In these organizations mayors and other officials can establish productive relationships with counterparts in other cities. In the months of the pandemic, Zoom and other similar innovations facilitate group contacts among several individuals in the absence of safe air travel. This calls into question the need for large, internationally connected airports of major cities and the enormous investments that have been made in them. This has always been a major source of competitive advantage for cities such as New York, Chicago, Atlanta, Seattle, and Los Angeles. However, if this sort of travel and of airport are going to diminish in importance, this opens the way for medium and smaller sized cities to enter into competition for talented and skilled workers, dynamic company investments, and notoriety.

In the world of distance conferencing by Zoom-type communications, working from home, and freedom from time-consuming socializing and office politics, working in a smaller city has its advantages. As William Alonso tells us, smaller cities can "borrow size" from a larger city in proximity. (Alonso, p. 200) The cost of inputs from other firms will be the same as if the two firms were in close proximity, except for a somewhat higher cost of transportation. This cost may be offset by lifestyle advantages of the smaller city, and individuals working there may still have access, with a bit of inconvenience to the assets of the larger city such as its international airport and cultural assets. It should be self-evident that workers who choose to live and work in a smaller city would be experiencing an improvement in their quality of life.

It is clear that an economy with increased connectedness and less isolation can be a double-edged sword from the standpoint of quality of life. For those who master the intricacies of information and communication technology the ensuing rewards should lead to enhanced quality of life; however, for those who are left out, perhaps for reasons beyond their control, life may become decreasingly satisfying and rewarding and their quality of life will suffer.

EFFECTIVENESS OF GOVERNMENT

Effective governance (the taking of actions by government) involves the articulation, by government, of a plan for future actions and policy, a design for their realization, mobilization of public support and the talents and resources that are required for realization of the plans, and gaining feedback from the residents of the city. An effective government is the *sine qua non* of a city having the urban amenities discussed in Chapter 5 – good public schools and healthcare, public security, congenial neighborhoods, good recreation and cultural facilities, and public transportation. In addition to having a vision and a masterplan, the city also needs regulations, investments, expenditures and incentives. (Rose, p. 139) This set of instruments unfortunately has often generated corruption on the part of the officers of the city and the state governments. The history of cities such as New Orleans, Detroit, and Chicago testify to this, as does the fact that three of Illinois' recent governors have spent time in prison for corruption of one sort or another. To make things worse, this corruption is also often accompanied with racial discrimination, housing segregation and other structural barriers to the advancement of those who are not favored by the corrupt officials. (Rose, p. 351.)

This need for effective government is taking place during a period of time in which the role of the national government and the revenues it can transfer to city government are shrinking. Less than a decade ago, Allen Scott wrote that major cities can no longer count on the central government to assist them in times of distress or to work with them to promote local economic development, and that "cities are now increasingly finding that they need to take much of the initiative themselves". (Scott, p. 167) The current plight of city and state governments in the midst of the pandemic is a clear example of the difficulties that confront lower level governments, many of which are constrained by statute from departing from a balanced annual budget. The current federal government in Washington opposes funding municipal governments because the cities are largely Democratic in their politics and neither the White House, that is the President, nor the Senate will fund a transfer of funds to city administrations. The result will most likely be a substantial reduction in the city and state government employment in many cases. This just illustrates the unreliability of multi-level government finances in the country today.

Jordi Borja and Manual Castells remind us that the growth in recent decades of the size of cities, and the complexity of them as structures of dozens or scores of smaller municipalities "multiplies the quality of life problems and increases the city residents and users' demands for social well-being". (Borja and Castells, p. 190) The evolving governing structures make this coordination increasingly difficult. Charles Landry illustrates this using Memphis as an example. Cities on the periphery of Memphis lobbied for infrastructure to give them access to the center of the city. This destroyed the integrity and shape of the city and induced some higher income residents to move from Memphis to one of the outlying cities. "This is a triple whammy. Memphis has to maintain its services on a lower income base, the city loses its mix of rich and poor, and the outer suburbanites exploit the bits of Memphis they like, such as using cultural facilities, while making little or no financial contribution to its maintenance. Only a metropolitan approach can solve this." (Landry, p. 296) This is exactly what Indianapolis has done by merging, in 1970, with Marion County to form Unigov, an entity that encompasses most of the Indianapolis MSA in a one mayor-council governmental structure headed by the mayor of the city. While not perfect, any more so than other human institutions, it is generally agreed that this has been a successful solution to the sort of problems that confront Memphis and many other US cities. (Wachter) A similar structure was created by Nashville and by Jacksonville. Absence of such a metro government makes it difficult to do metro wide planning. Both Chicago and London have had great difficulty in reconfiguring their airports in the face of resistance from smaller independent communities.

For a final word we can turn to Bruce Katz and Jennifer Bradley who, in their book *The Metropolitan Revolution*, criticize the federal and state levels of government as being "hyper political and partisan, hopelessly fragmented and compartmentalized, frustratingly bureaucratic, and prescriptive". Cities, on the other hand, are action oriented, they deal with innovation, imagination, and push boundaries; they "run businesses, provide services, educate children, train workers, build homes, and develop community … They reward leaders who push the envelope, catalyze action, and get stuff done". (Katz and Bradley, p. 7) Obviously enthusiasts, but, writing as a resident of Pennsylvania, their laudatory comments do appear to me to capture the essence of federal, state and metropolitan activities today.

FINAL THOUGHTS

Cities have seven principal attributes that have an impact on the quality of life of their residents. In this chapter we have examined each of the seven and have detailed the impact each has on quality of life. As we have noted, some consequences of each attribute will have positive impacts, while others will be negative in their impact. In these final comments we will focus on some of the more salient of their impacts.

Civic pride and the city's image or renown are linked in the minds of city residents, although pride in one's neighborhood can offset an image of a city in decline. In the city we create our own world based on the characteristics of the neighborhood, as well as the attributes of the city such as its cultural institutions, sports teams, retail options, and social spaces. Pride in one's neighborhood brings with it a responsibility to maintain the quality of our personal living space. A bit of decline can bring on the "broken windows" phenomenon, while small-thinking pride can bring with it ethnic or racial animosity and discrimination or at least a tolerance for them. A reputation for this sort of discrimination can have a powerfully negative impact on the city's image throughout the country and more.

Architecture and imaginative spaces are the image of the city to the rest of the world, as well as being a powerful element in the civic pride of its residents. We have seen how an architectural element can go wrong, as in St. Louis with the Gateway Arch, or positively, as in Santa Fe and many other cities. It can capture the real or imagined essence of a city and can serve as a guide to the city's leaders and institutions when they plan for the city's future and its relationship with other entities. Columbus, Indiana, is universally regarded as a city that has managed this brilliantly. All the "Great" cities of the world have worked on their image through outstanding architecture and public parks and other spaces. Imaginative architects and city planners, such as Vaux, Olmstead, Le Courbusier, and Burnham have left their imagination imprinted on the cities with which they worked. Others have focused on architecture and public spaces as powerful elements in the rebirth or recovery of a city that had gone into decline. These attributes can have a transformative impact on the quality of life of the city's residents.

How big should a city be? There is no answer to this question. We have demonstrated that bigger is not necessarily better, and also that smallness is not necessarily a deterrent to establishing a successful city or town. While there are certain obvious advantages to being a large city with its commercial and retail center, its international airport, its variety of residential options, and its cultural and recreational facilities, commuting, and gentrification in a growing city, are widely regarded disadvantages of size. Smaller cities and towns do have lifestyle advantages for a substantial portion of the population; there are some advantages in working from a small city or town. Furthermore, the consequences in the longer term of the pandemic may tilt the advantage away from large, crowded cities to more manageable smaller cities and towns. Alonso went so far as to suggest that small cities and towns could "borrow size" from larger cities in proximity, with the cost of transportation of industrial components offset by savings from location in a smaller place and some lifestyle benefits. Landry and Scott concurred that smaller places can be as competitive as their larger counterparts, especially in creativity and the new cognitive-cultural economy.

In this cognitive-cultural economy, connectedness by means of information and communications technologies is crucial for cities as well as for individuals. A crucial element here is the access to these technologies that students in all income classes and neighborhoods have. Deprivation in this regard is likely to condemn a young person to a life of marginalization and deprivation. It is the obligation of the society as a whole to ensure that all young people have the opportunity to develop their skills and talents fully, or that society will have to live with the consequences of its lack of concern today.

It is equally important for city leaders to be connected with their counterparts elsewhere, not just through telecommunications but through participation in organizations that bring them together to share ideas, problems and thoughts about solutions to problems. Mayors such as Chicago's Rahm Emmanuel have written impressively and passionately about the necessity of this interaction among mayors and senior policy personnel in the creative conduct of the city's business.

Without effective government, none of the quality of life enhancing attributes of a city would be achievable. The city leaders must undertake initiatives that will work toward this end; sadly, this often gives rise to the political corruption and crime that have characterized some of our cities. A free press and news media are essential elements in the control and deterrence of this crime. As was noted, this crime is often linked with other urban evils such as residential segregation and racial and ethnic discrimination. A major problem for cities, certainly in the period of the pandemic, is the precarious financial situation faced by most of our cities. Lacking a functioning partner in Washington, many cities will be obligated to lay off many of their employees, given their statutory constraint against deficit spending, even in a period such as this. As a response to many of the local difficulties in polity implementation and financial viability, many cities have pursued reforms such as metro-wide governance. This is not a solution for all cities, but it does give evidence to the creativity in our cities when mayors pursue initiatives such as this.

REFERENCES

Alonso, William, "Urban zero population growth", in Mancur Olson and Hans H. Landsburg, (eds), *The No Growth Society*, Abingdon: Frank Cass, pp. 191–206.

Ashworth, Gregory and Mihalis Kavaratzis, (eds), *Towards Effective Place Brand Management*, Cheltenham, UK and Northampton, MA, USA: Edward Elgar, 2010.

Begovic, Boris, "The Economic Approach to Optimal City Size", *Progress in Planning*, Vol. 36, No. 2, pp. 94–161.

Borja, Jordi and Manual Castells, *Local & Global, Management of Cities in the Information Age*, London: Earthscan Publications, 1996.

Camagni, Roberto, Roberta Capello and Andrea Caragliu, "The Rise of Second-rank Cities: What Role for Agglomeration Economies?", *European Planning Studies*, Vol. 23, No. 6, pp. 1069–89.

Campbell, Tracy, *The Gateway Arch*, New Haven: Yale University Press, 2013.

Collins, Tom, "Urban Civic Pride and the New Localism", *Transactions of the Institute of British Geographers*, Vol. 41, 2016, pp. 175–86.

Creative City Network, "Building Community Identity and Pride", *Making the Case for Culture*, Canada Council for the Arts. www.creativecity.ca.

Goldberger, Paul, "Miracle above Manhattan", *National Geographic*, April 2011. www .ngm.com.

Jaffee, Eric, "Why Commute Times Don't Change Much Even as a City Grows", *CityLab*, 20 June 2014. www.citylab.com.

Katz, Bruce and Jennifer Bradley, *The Metropolitan Revolution*, Washington: The Bookings Institution Press, 2013.
Kranton, Rachel, Seth Sanders and Matthew Pease, "Desire to be in a Group Leads to Harsher Judgement of Others: It's Not the Politics, it's the 'Groupiness' that Drives Discrimination", *ScienceDaily*, 18 August 2020. www.sciencedaily.com/released/2020/08/2008180941.htm.
Kresl, Peter Karl and Daniele Ietri, *Creating Cities/Building Cities*, Cheltenham, UK and Northampton, MA, USA: Edward Elgar, 2017.
Landry, Charles, *The Art of City Making*, London: Earthscan, 2006.
Moskowitz, Peter, *How to Kill a City*, New York: Nation Books, 2017.
Nikitin, Cynthia, "Civic Buildings and Their Public Spaces Can Improve the Quality of Life in Cities", *Recreation & Parks BC Magazine*, Spring 2009, pp. 10–11.
OECD, *Competitive Cities in the Global Economy*, Territorial Reviews, Paris: Organization for Economic Cooperation and Development, 2006.
Polito, William, "Pride Lacking in City Residents", *Altoona Mirror*, 3 June 2015.
Power, Anne, Jörg Plöger and Astrid Winkler, *Phoenix Cities: The Fall and Rise of Great Industrial Cities*, Bristol: The Policy Press, 2010.
Rentschler, Ruth, Kerrie Bridson and Jody Evans, *Civic Pride and Community Identity, The Impact of the Arts in Regional Australia, Stats and Stories – Theme 4*, Warrnambool: Deakin University, 2015.
Rose, Jonathan F. P., *The Well-Tempered City*, New York: HarperCollins, 2016.
Rybczynski, Witold, *Makeshift Metropolis: Ideas about Cities*, New York: Scribner, 2010.
Scott, Allen J., *A World in Emergence, Cities and Regions in the 21st Century*, Cheltenham, UK and Northampton, MA, USA: Edward Elgar, 2012.
Tate, Alan, *Great City Parks*, Abingdon: Spoon Press, 2001.
Wachter, Jeff, *40 Years After Unigov: Indianapolis and Marion County's Experience with Consolidated Government*, Baltimore: Abell Foundation, May 2014.
Wilson, James Q. and George L. Kelling, "Broken Windows", *Atlantic Monthly*, Vol. 249, No. 3, March 1982.

7. Urban amenities and quality of life

It has been an argument of this work that urban amenities are largely determinative of a city's quality of life. Others items, such as aspects of the economy and a city's attributes have been examined in previous chapters. But the central element is amenities. For a definition of amenities we can turn to the *Oxford Compact English Dictionary*, where we find that an amenity is "1) a pleasant or useful feature, or 2) pleasantness (of a place, etc.)". (Thompson, p. 29) We will argue here that there are eight amenities, or pleasant features, that are central to a city's quality of life: (1) congenial neighborhoods, (2) social services (3) good public education, (4) access to recreation facilities, (5) cultural institutions, (6) municipal transportation, (7) public security, and (8) suitable or quality housing. Each of them will be discussed in order below. But first we must examine some of the other approaches to the issue of amenities.

One of the principle alternatives to these eight is that the primary amenity has been the effect of climate or, specifically, of warm temperature; however its strength as an amenity and its impact on competitiveness are not as clear as has been proposed. We discovered from the findings of the UN Happiness Report, in Chapter 2, that the happiest populations live in northern and colder countries such as the five Nordic countries, Switzerland, the Netherlands, and Canada. Partridge, supporting Philip Grave's natural amenity migration model, reports that a city in a non-metropolitan county with Detroit's temperature should have a population growth that is 135 percent lower than one of Orlando's. For larger MSAs the figure is roughly 750 percent lower. Data were for the period 1950–2000. The average January and July temperatures are taken as proxies for, and indicators of the growth in, natural amenities. David Maddison and Katrin Rehdanz take a somewhat different approach to this question and generate results that are rather different than those of Partridge. They rate subjective wellbeing (SWB) as measured for residents of 165 countries, not cities, for the period 2005–15. The variables consist of five weather, three population, and three economic variables. They find the weather variables to be the best predictor of wellbeing, but not in the way Partridge does. Their results indicate a strong preference for less extreme temperatures, and that "climates where monthly temperatures are often below 18.3 degrees C (65 degrees Fahrenheit) strongly reduce SWB, as do those where monthly temperatures are often above 18.3 C. The farther temperatures deviate from 18.3 C, above or below, the greater is the reduction in SWB". (Maddison and

Rehdanz, p. 120) If we think of cities, this suggests that both Phoenix and Minneapolis-St. Paul would have lower SWB than, say, Denver.

However, it is of interest to note that Peter Karl Kresl and Balwant Singh demonstrated that, between the two periods 1977–87 and 1987–92, this was not the case. (Kresl and Singh, pp. 1020–21) Using growth of retail sales, growth of manufacturing value added and the growth of business services receipts as indicators of a city's competitiveness, of five regional groupings of cities, the strongest performing was the Industrial Triangle (Pittsburgh–Milwaukee–St. Louis), in which six MSAs grew between the two periods, with only Cleveland declining. In the Center, all grew (Dallas-Fort Worth, Denver, Minneapolis-St. Paul and Phoenix) except Kansas City which indicated no change. On the Pacific Coast, only Seattle grew in competitiveness, with Los Angeles, San Diego and San Francisco declining. In the South, Tampa grew but Miami and Atlanta declined. The four cities in the North East, Boston, Baltimore, Philadelphia, and New York, all declined. Clearly, with Miami, Atlanta, San Diego, and Los Angeles losing competitiveness and with Chicago, Pittsburgh and Minneapolis-St. Paul gaining, temperature and golf courses had little to do with urban competitiveness, nor perhaps with amenities. Furthermore, until the recent injection of high tech and financial services into cities such as Atlanta, Charlotte and Orlando, and the Research Triangle, much of the migration of population to the South consisted of retirees. This was true for the period 1977–92 and for a specific definition of urban competitiveness, but in the context of Partridge, and Maddison and Rehdanz, it does make the point.

In a similar vein, McCann, reviewing literature on amenities in European cities finds cities in the North and West rate higher than do those in the South and East. He concludes that "within Europe it appears that quality of life issues are more closely related to the quality of governance and institutional issues than to natural climate-related issues". (McCann, 2015, p. 44) Similarly, in US cities, climate is nested in a complex of other more powerful determinants, such as healthcare, proximity to one or more universities, restaurants, culture and music, and college or professional sports teams. Cities listed as "top ten" in various ratings, such as Austin, or Raleigh-Durham-Chapel Hill have warmer temperatures but also the just mentioned attributes, as do Minneapolis-St. Paul, Boston and Seattle and Madison which lack the warm climate of Austin or the Research Triangle.

The Knight Foundation conducted a project, "Knight Soul of the Community 2010", in which they examined the issue of why people have strong attachments to a certain place, and conclude that the report "proves that a significant connection exists between residents' levels of emotional attachment to their community and its economic growth". (Knight Foundation, p. 2)

They found that three items mattered most in city after city and in year after year: social offerings, openness and aesthetics. The latter includes things such as nightlife, culture and arts, openness to people of all preferences and beliefs, availability of parks and trails, beauty of the physical setting of the city, and ease of meeting people. Absent from the top listing were economy, civic involvement, leadership, education, and basic services; weather or climate were not considered. (Knight, pp. 9–11) The top amenities were clearly quality of life issues rather than 'hard' economic and political issues.

It must be stressed that amenities are not a magic bullet that will turn any place into a highly desirable one for the educated and mobile workforce on which we are focused. It does work for some places and at some times, but certainly not for others. Thirty years ago, Paul Gottlieb wrote, in an economy of services and engineering, that the proprietor choosing a facility location will select one that will maximize his or her "psychic income", even if profit is not maximized. Furthermore, a staff of technical professionals will leave for another facility unless the location of the facility "has a high quality of life and amenities that appeal to a managerial elite". He pointedly concludes that "development officials and researchers ignore the provision of *residential* amenities at their peril". (Gottlieb, pp. 271–81) While this was a different economy than the one we have today, the point is still relevant.

Finally, the argument has been that it is jobs and not amenities that motivate labor movement, and it has been noted that students come from home in one place, go to university in another, and then move on for the job; they do not move for amenities. But my students had job offers from several employers, so it was not "take this job or nothing". They moved to a great variety of places and my experience was that amenities did play a role in their decision. But, of course, a large city is a combination of a variety of attractive amenities as well as being at the center of "the action" in a sector of the economy. Bjørn Asheim and Høgni Kalsø Hansen used three knowledge-based categories of labor – analytical (science-based), synthetic (engineering-based) and symbolic (arts-based) – and found that synthetic-based labor responded best with regard to "business climate" variables, while analytical and most strongly symbolic-based workers were most responsive to "people climate" variables. (Asheim and Hansen) This is in general conformity with what one understands of the lifestyle preferences of engineers and of performing artists! The economists I know would throw their lot in with the latter.

With this introductory material behind us, we can now examine each of the eight individual amenities that are so powerfully linked to quality of life in a city.

CONGENIAL NEIGHBORHOODS

Everyone prefers to live in a neighborhood that is inhabited with people who are friendly, with parks, good retail outlets, grocery stores, restaurants, and bars and other social spaces. This is true of younger tech workers and is even truer when they have families with younger children. Streets should have sidewalks, traffic should be slow, noise should be under control, playgrounds should give children a place to play other than on streets, and trees and other plantings should soften the prospect and the feel of the place.

One of the classic articles about congenial neighborhoods was that by James Wilson and George Kelling in which they introduced us to the notion of "Broken Windows". (Wilson and Kelling) They noted that in any neighborhood if there was a building or a car with a broken window, so that it looked abandoned, some individuals would cause further damage to the thing with the broken window, and that before long the car or building would be totally stripped of anything of value. If the window were fixed so the entity looked as though someone took care of it, this stripping would not occur, or at least not as quickly. In Newark, New Jersey, the city began to take police out of squad cars and have them walk the streets. Officers got to know the residents, and they the police. The police were able to ascertain who belonged in the neighborhood and who did not. Police on foot managed to make the neighborhood less frightening and a friendlier place for local residents. Having the police visible and on foot made the residents feel that the neighborhood was safer, and more congenial. While research actually showed this action did not reduce crime, it made the residents feel that it had.

Here the important thing was to make the neighborhood into a more pleasant place in which to live, to walk, to shop and to socialize – a place that enhanced their perception of their quality of life. Objectively, they were not better off, but subjectively they perceived themselves to be so. While this is not everything, it is something of value.

Unfortunately, "congenial" has had less salubrious implications in many or most US cities and the definition of congenial came to mean living with others with whom one felt comfortable. In cities throughout the country this means keeping out those with whom one did not feel comfortable, people who were not of the "right" race, color, religion, ethnic origin, political persuasion, sexual orientation, or even age. This was developed into a fine art by the real estate industry with innovations such as red-lining, restrictive covenants, zoning and other measures designed to enhance the "quality of life" of white residents, often of at least a specific minimal income. Mortgages were not available to non-whites in many places, apartment buildings that would appeal to lower income residents were forbidden, and in Portland, Oregon, owning or occupying a building in "congenial" neighborhoods was precluded for "Chinese, Japanese, Italians, Greeks, Hindus, Armenians, Indians, Mexicans and Negros". (Smith, pp. 358 and 360) African Americans were confined to limited areas, with no access to loans or mortgages so their houses could not be maintained and deteriorated over time until they were razed for urban renewal and the residents were parked in high rise buildings, after their neighborhood and all of the attendant social relations had been destroyed.

Hence, one person's "congenial" became another's "deprivation". Sadly, enhancing the quality of life for one group can lead to its destruction for another.

SOCIAL SERVICES

The social services offered by city governments are many and are diverse. Public education is one of the primary services a city can offer and it is significant enough for us to treat it separately in the section that follows this one. Police and fire will be discussed below in the Public Security section. The remaining social services include: healthcare, subsidized housing, job training, child protective care, food subsidies, policy research, and lobbying with higher levels of government for funding and for support in providing other services. The pandemic that is raging during 2020 and into 2021 brought heightened attention to the community's needs for city supervision and support of healthcare, food banks, housing assistance, child protection and coordination with other levels of government – in short, almost all of the services just listed.

In normal times, food banks, subsidized housing, childcare, and job training are used by residents with lower incomes. However, during the pandemic and the attendant economic collapse many middle income individuals and families found it necessary to avail themselves of these public services. We saw lines of $35,000 SUVs inching toward a distribution point for bags of groceries, presumably with families who were availing themselves of this service for the first time in their life. Individuals of all income levels were taken to the same hospitals. They also lined up for COVID-19 testing, and relied upon local authorities to impose masking and social distancing mandates. Renters who lost their employment were often evicted from their house or apartment and had to avail themselves of the limited number of subsidized public housing alternatives. The pandemic has increased the appreciation of all residents for the provision of social services by the local government. State and local governments have an increased interest in lobbying the federal government for additional resources so they can provide these sorely needed services. The current government in Washington is not responsive to these needs, but if there is a change in government in 2021 this situation could improve significantly for these governments and, of course, for the residents who will benefit from provision of these services.

The objectives of provision of social services are the building of community, countering the consequences of extreme differences in personal or family income, enhancing employment opportunities, enhancing the quality of local government services, and, in general, increasing the quality of life of all city residents.

GOOD PUBLIC EDUCATION

Public education here refers to pre-K through high school (grade 12). The quality of this is obviously of great concern to young workers with younger children. Historically, this has been sought by immigrant families who understand that access to the mainstream of American society and economy is predicated on success in a high quality program of education. They do not find the alternative road to material wellbeing, crime, to be at all attractive.

How we deal with quality of public education depends on the society in which our study takes place. In most countries there is a national system of education with standardized courses, syllabi and examinations. One thinks of students around the world taking the same examination at the same time for entry into, say, the French or UK university system. There is less pressure then for parents to choose to live in a particular city or neighborhood to gain access to higher quality education than could be found elsewhere. Indeed, in one study of quality of life in Britain, the top elements are two indicators of crime, one of health services, low pollution levels, cost of living, racial harmony, and shopping facilities; education was only one of 20 variables used and this was just pupil/teacher ratio in primary and in secondary schools. (Finlay, et al., pp. 271 and 273) US universities, by contrast, admit students based on a variety of qualities, including high school academic record, scores in standard tests such as the SAT or the ACT, an essay, an interview, activities done in and out of school, and several other items. Hence, in the US it can matter greatly whether a student is enrolled in a school that offers an excellent education or one that is average or mediocre. One's working life, and life in general, can depend heavily on the quality of education through high school to which a student has access.

We noted Putnam's linking between access to good schooling and success later in life, with success referring to standard indicators of success, such as life employment, family life, and essentially the ability to be an active decision maker rather than a passive acceptor of what life chooses to give to one. (Putnam, ch. 6) Many students, and their families, are trapped in residential areas in which they have to tolerate sub-standard educational facilities and opportunities. Policies such as transporting students to school in buses simply have not been able to overcome the disadvantages given to students in red-lined, ghettoized and marginal residential areas. Families of the "right" color and the "right" income can have access to schooling that will propel their children forward, and upward; students lacking this will be condemned to less successful working lives. Hence the struggle to get into the right school district.

ACCESS TO RECREATION FACILITIES

The workers who are most sought after in today's economy, are younger and more educated than was the case in the past. They tend to be active physically and seek to attain and to maintain a level of fitness and health that makes recreational spaces and facilities important to them. Many of them are engaged in running, walking, trail hiking, mountain hiking, exercise in fitness centers or gymnasiums, and swimming. They accompany this physical activity with carefully thought-out plans for diet and eating. Naturally, they are attracted to cities that offer opportunities for engaging in these activities, in many cases this is a *sine qua non*. Hence, city and company officials not only have to offer this to potential workers, they also have to invest funds and land into recreation and physical fitness facilities. Cities such as Denver, Seattle, Minneapolis-St. Paul, and Salt Lake City are renowned for their success in this area. But other cities such as Chicago, Atlanta, Boston and San Francisco have their own recreation offerings. It has also become the case that young workers who are perfectly willing to telecommute, or to work from home, are moving to smaller cities in places where recreation spaces can be found. Billings (Montana), Durango (Colorado), Burlington (Vermont), Eugene (Oregon), and Flagstaff (Arizona) are all smaller cities that attract younger people because of their outdoor recreational possibilities.

Richard Florida raised this issue in 2002 when he wrote that: "Creative Class people ... are drawn to places and communities where many outdoor activities are prevalent – both because they enjoy these activities, and because their presence is seen as a signal that the place is amenable to the broader creative lifestyle". He notes that higher income people are most likely to engage in active sports, while those with a lower income are drawn to spectator sports. (Florida, p. 173) David McGranahan, Timothy Wojan and Dayton Lambert found that outdoor amenities are related to a higher rate of economic growth because: (1) they have higher proportions of creative class members, (2) they are associated with entrepreneurship, and (3) in higher amenity cities footloose businesses will be attracted because of the synergistic effects of entrepreneurship and creative class members. (McGranahan, et al., p. 539) They found that the synergistic relationship between creative class, entrepreneurial activity and outdoor amenities has had a powerful impact on US rural growth, but that this synergy was related to the strength of the outdoor amenities at hand. This type of growth that is based on attracting creative people as residents is more sustainable than that based on growth of fee-paying tourist guests. Availability of fiber optic cable is a *sine qua non* of such a strategy, for without it creative people will not come. One possible shortcoming would be that creative people might be tempted to close the door to newcomers so as to preserve the access to recreational assets they have found. (McGranahan, et al., p. 270)

In spite of a reservation or two, we are left with the understanding that access to recreational facilities enhances quality of life and is an important element in attracting and retaining a younger, educated labor force, especially those who have families.

CULTURAL INSTITUTIONS

In Chapter 3, we discussed the impact of cultural institutions on a city's economy and competitiveness. Here we will take a second look at this sector and how it relates to a city's quality of life. At that time, we referred to the report done by the Port Authority of New York and New Jersey in 2019, but there was another report that preceded it by a quarter of a century. In that 1993–94 report Part II is focused on Tourism and Travel to the region, but Part I is "The Arts as an Industry", and discusses the economic importance of culture. It is instructive to compare the number of cultural institutions in three US cities, NYC, LA and Chicago, as early as 1992: commercial galleries – 481, 115, 89; museums – 49, 33, 19; commercial theaters – 34, 4, 9; symphony orchestras – 26, 20, 13; and opera companies – 14, 5, 7 respectively. Of course, Los Angeles dominates in film and recording services. (The Port Authority, Appendix A) Between 1992 and 2017, employment in New York's cultural industries grew from 107,000 to 293,365, and now exceeds employment in sectors such as finance and banking. The creative economy is increasingly a major component of the knowledge economy, as is shown by the decline of employment in fashion production by 43 percent between 2008 and 2017, and an increase in fashion design of 27 percent – an increase that was second only to advertising and film and television.

Elizabeth Currid wrote that: "Culture is often treated as an amenity, and thus a lure for professionals and workers in other industries who want to live and work in a culturally vibrant place". (Currid, p. 46) It has clearly been central to the strength of the New York economy and the attractiveness of well-paid, educated staff in sectors other than culture and the arts. This has been vital to economies of New York and other major cities, as many traditional strengths of their economies, such as wholesale trade and manufacturing, have left and resituated themselves in other, usually, lower cost places. The primary force behind this has been the advances in technology, information, and transportation that forced company decision-makers to relocate to survive. The growth of the employment and revenues of the cultural industries has both provided vitality to these established urban economies and has made them more attractive, through the creation of amenities and higher quality of life, to other industries that grew in the new tech economy of the 21st century and replaced the firms that moved on. One of the attractive features of the suburbs that ring these established cultural center cities, and offer corporate "campuses", is the easy access residents have to the city's cultural attractions – orchestras, theaters, dance companies, and museums, by means of convenient rail or other means of travel.

As Landry tells us: "Creativity has risen because people have realized that the sources of competitiveness now happen on a different plane and they need to learn afresh how to compete beyond merely low cost and high productivity. It includes a city's cultural depth and richness, which might mean heritage or the a availability of contemporary artistic facilities". (Landry, pp. 391–2) A city's cultural assets are an essential ingredient in any competitive urban economy in the economy of the 21st century. Its employees are well educated, and sooner or later they seek engagement with art, music, dance and theater, even if only for the education of their children. James Heilbrun and Charles Gray have written that while businessmen, in 1993 at least, consider quality of life variables to be climate, public safety, and education, they do recognize that culture creates a favorable image of the city. Their financial contributions to the community are made out of recognition that this is a way of "making the local community a better place in which to live … and because they make an indispensable contribution to the wellbeing of the women and men who make up the local community". (Heilbrun and Gray, p. 322) Either way, cultural assets are a powerful amenity and contributor to quality of life.

MUNICIPAL TRANSPORTATION

The geographic space of American cities has for the past 150 years been powerfully determined by public expenditures on transportation. In Chapter 2 we discussed the close proximity of place of work and place of residence for industrial workers in the 19th century. As the industrial revolution extended to modes of transportation, innovations such as railroads, trams and streetcars, as well as ferries, facilitated a growing percentage of the population to escape the smoke and pollution and squalor of the industrial sectors into empty lands that surrounded the city. The transportation system was virtually fully implemented by the end of the century. The suburbs were generally developed by a developer or corporation that would manage the various aspects of that suburb. Earlier in this chapter we discussed the income discrimination and racial segregation that were features of these suburbs. Some suburbs were inhabited by very wealthy families with close proximity to golf courses and green spaces, but with an easy commute to the central business district. New York developed suburbs that were served by ferry and steam railroads. Philadelphia developed suburbs along the Mail Line of the Pennsylvania

Railroad. Chicago, the transportation center of the country, had 11 rail lines serving over 100 suburbs by the time of the Great Fire in 1871. Virtually every large city in the US had its rail and streetcar serviced suburbs, by the first years of the 20th century. By this time, streetcars had been elevated in New York and Chicago, and in a few years subway systems were developed that replaced some elevated systems. Most systems were built by the municipality and then operated by private companies. By World War II municipalities had begun to take over operation of the systems.

This process was, of course, managed by municipal governments, and usually with a substantial subsidy. This subsidy was in support of families with sufficient income to support the move, and that were acceptable to suburb developers and their discriminatory practices. Those left behind could not benefit from this support. Those who could make the move to the suburbs were also able to benefit from access to a mortgage and FHA support. Additionally they were given a substantial benefit from the tax deductibility of mortgage interest payments. In the words of Ed Glaeser, "That subsidy makes owning cheaper than renting, and being pro-home-ownership means being anticity". (Glaeser, p. 194) Thus, whether municipal support of transportation is a quality of life enhancing amenity depends upon the extent to which one can take advantage of it, or is left behind.

PUBLIC SECURITY

Public security encompasses law enforcement (police), fire departments and emergency medical services. While police services are provided by the state, the county and the municipality, the other two tend to be provided solely by the municipality. Emergency medical services are provided to transport individuals who need hospital treatment from wherever they are to the hospital, be it a home or a car or the road or a place of recreation. This tends to be non-controversial, except when the emergency unit will not serve some location because of a local situation which they perceive to be dangerous. Fire departments generally service any location to which they are called, perhaps because they travel in large vehicles and usually have a large team of firemen and are more protected than are emergency medical units. All residents of a city or town have very positive impressions of these two services and one could say that they serve to enhance the quality of life for virtually all residents.

The same cannot be said of police services. We noted above, in the discussion of "broken windows", that when Newark replaced patrol cars with officers on foot the perception of the impact on residents' quality of life was enhanced. So how police officers carry out their duty does have an impact on the perceptions of the residents with regard to the impact on their quality of life. This has become all too clear this past year (2020) when African American residents rose up against the actions of police officers towards, among others, a young teenager playing with a water pistol, a woman, Breonna Taylor, who was killed in her bed during a non-warrant incursion into her apartment at midnight; several other Black men were killed in situations that range from the clear murder of George Floyd in Minneapolis to Rayshard Brooks in Atlanta, who was armed with an officer's taser and was running away. From the perspective of police officers, the suspect is unknown to them and may very well be armed, and, having encountered many very dangerous situations, they may be risk averse. From the perspective of Black Lives Matter and many dispassionate television viewers the issue is often not at all clear cut. One suspects that today far fewer parents teach their children "the policeman is a friend of mine …".

In this instance, police services do enhance the quality of life of the majority of citizens but for many others, of color, this is no longer true. Rectifying this situation is one of the major challenges that will be faced by city governments in the coming years. One of the primary positions taken is that we have loaded up the police forces with responsibilities for the homeless, drug addicts, family conflict, runaway children, the mentally disturbed, and drug trafficking, among other things. One approach, that has been misunderstood and misrepresented is that of reformulating the responsibilities of police forces to be limited to crime, and to transfer the other tasks, and the funding that attaches to them, to social workers, medical facilities, and other specialists who are better prepared to offer these services in a less confrontational and more effective manner. This would diminish the number of residents in a city who felt that police services diminish their quality of life and increase the number of those who view the police in a positive light.

SUITABLE OR QUALITY HOUSING

Earlier in this chapter we noted the mixed impact local governments and the real estate industry they supported had on the availablility of quality housing for all elements in the community. Red-lining and restrictive covenants precluded many residents from obtaining a mortgage and home ownership, the principal element of wealth of all but the wealthiest residents. We also noted that one of the services provided by local government is subsidized housing. The history of local government and housing is thus a mixed one. Recently, however, pressure has been building for local government to do more to redress the mal-intended actions of past decades with policies and actions to, for example, allow multiple occupancy apartment buildings in all parts of the city. Minneapolis-St. Paul has been perhaps the first major city to end the requirement of single-family housing with its Minneapolis 2040 plan. This is designed to increase the number of affordable housing units in the city and to reverse a history of racist housing policy. Duplexes and triplexes will now be allowed in all neighborhoods. Similar projects are underway in Portland, Oregon and in Seattle. Perhaps a key to the success of Minneapolis is the fact that the Minneapolis City Council is composed of 12 Democrats and one Green Party member. Currently in the city 60 percent of whites own their home, while less than 25 percent of non-whites do. Mayor Frey commented that this plan was an effort "to allow for a beautiful diversity of people throughout our city and in every neighborhood". (Mervosh)

Awareness of the inequity of city housing policies over the past few decades has been brought to the attention of all by the 2020 reactions to police brutality with regard to Black young men. The entire relationship between the races has been examined and found to be in immediate need of corrective action and policy. In addition to discriminatory police practices, disadvantages in healthcare and in housing have become the subject of widespread discussion. Policies enacted in 2021 will be crucial in healing some of the deep wounds that have afflicted American social policy and society. Actions taken in this area will tend to enhance the quality of life of some previously discriminated against groups and will cause others to feel their quality of life has been diminished. In Minneapolis, one of the causes for reaction against Minneapolis 2040 is the fear that this will result in high rise apartment buildings encroaching into "family" neighborhoods in which that had been disallowed. Whether this fear is rational or just a justification to retain the existing racist housing policy will come to light in the future.

FINAL THOUGHTS

When we began our examination of amenities, we discovered that the simplest and seemingly most obvious ones were not supported by evidence. Warm weather is a classic example of this. We found that the issue of amenities and which of them were important to talented workers was more complex and subtly differentiated than had been thought. Different categories of worker found their quality of life to be positively impacted by different amenities. The same amenity, when introduced to a society that is complex and highly differentiated generates a dramatically different impact on quality of life, depending on the individual being considered and their life situation. This became clear when we examined the eight different amenities we selected for this chapter.

Some of them were affected by characteristics of American society, primarily by race and income. For example, congenial neighborhoods are the result of the development over time of a racist housing and settlement policy. A policy as innocuous as allowing only single family housing was instituted as a way to keep neighborhoods from being racially integrated and integrated with lower-income families. Equally contentious is the practice of police policy in the context of racial and income segregation – some neighborhoods are seen by police as being dangerous and require a rapid resort to techniques of rigorous control and submission of the resident. Obviously, mistakes can be made. Policies such as "three strikes and you're out" result in sentences that are close to life imprisonment and differential treatment of injecting crack cocaine and snorting powder results in dramatically different sentences for using one means of delivery of cocaine rather than another. Gradually, we are becoming aware of the often unintended consequences of policies such as these and efforts to reconsider them are under way. Neither fire departments nor emergency medical services have these negative aspects.

With education it is not that some have a positive and others a negative quality of life impact, it is rather that while some have a strongly positive impact, others are excluded from access to this amenity. This is largely due to the fact that public education is a local responsibility in the US and funded to a significant degree by the local authority. So some students have funding lavished upon them while others are deprived. In several states, including Vermont and Pennsylvania, movements to equalize funding for students in all schools were defeated by the opposition from voters in wealthier districts. Public education then is unable to accomplish its task of creating an educated population throughout the state. The impact of education on quality of life differs widely among students.

When we look at access to recreational facilities and to cultural institutions, the situation is quite different. These two activities tend to be targeted at the more highly educated and younger population. So clearly the impact on the quality of life in both instances is positive, while many others are left out. But there should be no negative impact on the quality of life of these others as the impact on the economy of these two amenities that draw a highly pro-ductive workforce to the city will have significant positive spillovers to the rest of the population. The economy should be stronger, employment should be increased, incomes all around will probably rise and all residents should benefit, albeit not necessarily directly.

Finally, local government housing policy has been a contentious issue in most places. Public transportation opened the areas beyond the city itself to development, but it was controlled by private entities and real estate compa-nies so that housing became racially and income segregated. Some were left, trapped in the inner districts and isolated from the rest of the life of the city. Housing policy and policing are perhaps the two most contentious areas of city policy that are currently subject to reconsideration and to reform. Recent expe-riences of the African American population have generated strong movements, throughout society, for this reform.

In most of these areas the issue of quality of life has been received differ-ently by white and Black, and by rich and poor, residents. The challenge is clearly to introduce policy reforms that will enable all residents to experience a positive quality of life from city policies.

REFERENCES

Asheim, Bjørn and Høgni Kalsø Hansen, "Knowledge Bases, Talents, and Contexts: On the Usefulness of the Creative Class Approach in Sweden", *Economic Geography*, Vol. 85, pp. 425–42.

Currid, Elizabeth, *The Warhol Economy: How Fashion, Art, & Music Drive New York City*, Princeton: Princeton University Press, 2007.

Findlay, Allan, Arthur Morris and Robert Rogerson, "Where to Live in Britain in 1988", *Cities*, August 1988, pp. 268–76.

Florida, Richard, *The Rise of the Creative Class*, New York: Basic Books, 2002.

Glaeser, Ed, *Triumph of the City*, New York: The Penguin Press, 2011.

Gottlieb, Paul D., "Amenities as an Economic Development Tool: Is There Enough Evidence?", *Economic Development Quarterly*, Vol. 8, No. 3, August 1994, pp. 270–85.

Heilbrun, James and Charles M. Gray, *The Economics of Art and Culture: an American Perspective*, Cambridge: Cambridge University Press, 1993.

Knight Foundation, *Knight Soul of the Community 2010*, Miami: Knight Foundation, 2010.

Kresl, Peter Karl and Balwant Singh, "Competitiveness and the Urban Economy: Twenty-four Large US Metropolitan Areas", *Urban Studies*, Vol. 36, Nos. 5–6, pp. 1017–28.

Landry, Charles, *The Art of City Making*, London: Earthscan, 2006.

McGranahan, David A., Timothy R. Wojan, and Dayton M. Lambert, "The Rural Growth Trifecta: Outdoor Amenities, Creative Class and Entrepreneurial Context", *Journal of Economic Geography*, Vol. 11, No. 3, May 2001, pp. 529–57.

Maddison, David and Katrin Rehdanz, "Cross-country variations in subjective wellbeing explained by the climate", in David Maddison, Katrin Rehdanz and Heinz Welsch, (eds), *Handbook on Wellbeing, Happiness and the Environment*, Cheltenham, UK and Northampton, MA, USA: Edward Elgar, 2020.

McCann, Eugene, J., "'Best Places': Interurban Competition, Quality of Life and Popular Media Discourse", *Urban Studies*, Vol. 41, No. 10, September 2004, pp. 1909–29.

Mervosh, Sarah, "Minneapolis, Tackling Housing Crisis and Inequity, Votes to End Single-Family Zoning", *The New York Times*, 13 December 2018. https://nyti.ms/2ggo.IPO.

Partridge, Mark D., "The Dueling Models: NEG vs Amenity Migration in Explaining U.S. Engines of Growth", *Papers in Regional Science*, Vol. 89, No. 3, 2010, pp. 513–36.

Putnam, Robert, *Our Kids, The American Dream in Crisis*, New York: Simon and Schuster, 2015.

Smith, Greta, "'Congenial Neighbors': Restrictive Covenants and Residential Segregation in Portland, Oregon", *Oregon Historical Quarterly*, Vol. 119, No. 3, Fall 2018, pp. 358–64.

The Port Authority of NY and NJ, *The Arts as an Industry: Their Economic Importance to the New York-New Jersey Metropolitan Region*, The Port Authority of NY and NJ, October 1993.

Thompson, Della, (ed.), *The Oxford Compact English Dictionary*, Oxford: Oxford University Press, 1996.

Wilson, James Q. and George L. Kelling, "Broken Windows", *Atlantic Monthly*, Vol. 249, No. 3, March 1982.

8.   Looking forward

We have devoted our attention to quality of life and its impacts on major elements in the economy of a city and, reciprocally, how some major elements of that city have their impact on quality of life. Quality of life, itself, is not conceptually or definitionally fixed, but varies over time and in relation to the human beings who are living the lives. We could have discussed the definition of the term, quality of life, at the outset, but that would have been premature. By this time, most readers will have attempted to formulate their own notion of the quality of life. In this concluding chapter it might be useful to review some of the primary elements in quality of life, how they vary by circumstance over time, and what quality of life as a concept attempts to capture.

In order that we may gain an understanding of the subject, it is useful to turn, once again, to the *Oxford Compact English Dictionary*. Here we read that quality has three definitions that are useful to us: (1) the degree of excellence of a thing, (2) a general excellence as "their work has quality", and (3) a distinctive attribute or faculty. (Thompson, p. 822) So quality of life can be filled with satisfying elements or it may be disappointing. When seeking to deal with quality of life as a policy issue, city leaders seek to enhance the "excellence" of what they are offering to those who are motivated to seek out a quality of life that is satisfying to them – that they identify as "excellent". Naturally, our cities of today are constantly in a struggle to develop the largest set of satisfying elements that they possibly can, short of bankruptcy, of course! We have reviewed how this has changed over time as cities sought to develop economies with different characteristics. During the past half century we have transitioned from quality of life, being composed of "hard" factors, such as location of a body of water, proximity to a mine or other natural resource, transportation for the goods produced as well as for the material used in their fabrication, housing within walking distance of the mill or factory, and so forth, to being composed of "soft" factors, such as cultural and recreational facilities, public security, quality K-12 education, congenial neighborhoods, and the transportation system, whether public buses, rail and subways, or expressways, for the contemporary economy. Thus, while we can give a definition of the term itself – excellence in the individual elements in what is being offered by the city, its composition will evolve over the decades. Daniel Naud and Rémy Tremblay go so far as to write: "it is difficult to define what we mean by quality of life. In effect, it seems as though too often it is the researchers who define the term without taking into consideration the opinion of the residents of the cities they are studying." (Naud and Tremblay, p. 64)

Perhaps the most effective way to ascertain the relative quality of life of a city is to observe whether the desired workforce is attracted to the city and whether the city can retain them and their families. Failure in either one would indicate a low quality of life. Hence, any definition of quality of life must be composed of the factors or elements that are central to the economy of the day. The elements that comprise quality of life for manufacturing, retail and services, and high tech economies are, as has been shown in Chapter 4, dramatically different and even unique for each economy.

We have reviewed these relationships from multiple points of view, and some of the material was, as a consequence of this, close to being repetitive. This being the case, rather than review the points made in the text, it would seem to be more important at this date, in the midst of a coronavirus pandemic, to suggest some of the consequences of this pandemic that are most important to the economic life of major cities. How will a major city's quality of life be affected? What will be the consequences for the principal elements in the quality of life for the contemporary economy and the staff who comprise its enterprises?

The estimated duration of the pandemic is quite uncertain, and is as dependent upon successful administration of vaccines and other medical treatments, as it is on the development of effective leadership at the national level. By the time this book is being read, it can only be hoped that we have been successful in both regards. May we be reading this in happier and healthier times than is the case as it is being written.

IMPACTS OF THE CORONAVIRUS ON THE ECONOMY, AND ON QUALITY OF LIFE

The experience of the US with the virus has been unique, with the possible exception of Brazil, whose leader, President Bolsonaro, has responded with a degree of ineptitude that is quite similar to that of our President Trump. As is widely known, Mr. Trump at first ignored the virus, then he said it was minor and would have no significant impacts, then he said it would die in the heat of April, then he said it would simply disappear, and then he declined to share federal government stocks of medical gear and equipment with the states and cities and with their medical facilities. All the while, the numbers of cases and of deaths were rising until today we have more of each than does any other country. Mr. Trump wanted to downplay the severity of the virus, as that would have a negative impact on the economy and, more importantly, on his chances of re-election in November. All of this has been widely publicized and must be known to all readers of this book. Nonetheless, it had to be reiterated as an introduction to this examination of the impacts of the virus on US cities.

Before we examine the impacts of the coronavirus on the economy, it should be noted that the impact on most of the population will be sharply negative with regard to their quality of life. Nina Lakhani wrote in *The Guardian*, in August, that the failure of the Trump administration to renew enhanced federal unemployment and other benefits to support renters and small businesses will "contribute to a wave of despair, drug overdoses and suicides among Americans". To add to this, one official in Chicago, county board president Toni Preckwinkle, said that: "Disinvestment, red lining and systematic racism have culminated in a crisis that once again hits the African American community hardest". Several states refused to fund expansion of Medicaid. One official in Alabama stated that "The pandemic has exposed our crumbling mental health system, and the biggest struggle in doing this work is knowing that we're putting a band-aid over a gaping hole". (Lakhani) The Trump administration does not even recognize the problem let alone work to resolve it. In other words the "deaths of despair", of Case and Deaton, will return with a vengeance.

Neil Irwin offers a rather grim forecast for the post-virus economy for the US and its large cities. He notes that after the 2008 financial crisis, it took two years for bank failures to peak, and state and local governments cut employment until early 2013. Cutbacks in municipal funding are relatively easy to accomplish, but raising taxes to reestablish city coffers is another issue and may take years. When companies lay off workers, it will take several months, after an expansion begins, to find, hire, train and integrate their replacements. The collapse happens in a very short time, but a recovery will be sluggish and may take years to achieve its initial position of vitality. Irwin quotes Brookings Fellow Tracy Gordon as stating that: "The first year is not the worst in any crisis. It's the second year where you have to do the harder stuff". (Irwin)

One of the consequences of the virus is the decision of many major companies, such as Google, Twitter, other tech firms, and financial institutions to allow their employees to work from home. This decision is rich in implications. First, firms have discovered that productivity is either unchanged or actually higher when people work from home – no interruptions, or long lunches, or coffee breaks, or need to take time off for various things such as family emergencies, and so forth. Hence, many firms may be satisfied with having their staff telecommute for the foreseeable future. Second, with staff not in the office the need for costly downtown office space will be reduced. This is already having an impact on the commercial property market in many cities, large and small. Not only will property firms be hurt but so will their financial backers and banks as well, and it may take them years to recover. Third, fewer trips to the office will change significantly the demands of workers for public transportation and use of expressways. Decreased bus and subway ridership is already having financial impacts on metropolitan transit budgets, and fewer miles on cars mean that service visits will be reduced as will be the demand for new cars. Car producers and dealerships will both feel this impact. Air travel may not recover to its pre-virus levels until at least 2024. Fourth, a dearth of office workers in downtown districts will have a negative impact on the financial viability of the entire array of retail and entertainment establishments one finds there. In Chicago, it has been estimated that about 4,200 small businesses have been forced to close due to customers and their revenue; and that about half of them will close permanently. Nationwide, half of small business firms will also be shut down for good, and the workers laid off could take months or even years to find another job. The town center may never return to what it had become by the end of 2019. Finally, when staff work from home they are not in the office. This means that they come into contact with senior managers less often or not at all, and they don't learn how to navigate office bureaucratic structures. Both of these impacts will have a negative impact on opportunities for advancement and promotion in the hierarchy, and on their careers. Furthermore, it will be a negative consequence for the firm if staff are not in contact with one another to tacitly transfer the knowledge gained in the firm from senior to junior members. The impacts of working from home are more complex than initially thought and the impacts on staff careers must be carefully considered – will the best employees be discovered and promoted?

A further cautionary note is offered by Marc Frenette and Kristyn Frank, of the Institute for Research on Public Policy, in Canada. Asking who will be at risk due to the automation that firms are forecast to introduce as a response to the requirements of the pandemic years, they suggest that it will not just be those who are easily replaced on the production line and other labor intensive work. For Canadian workers, older workers and those with lower incomes or low literacy or numeracy have a job loss risk of greater than 70 percent, while those with a university degree have a risk of 2 percent. Those with a post-secondary degree in physical and life sciences and technologies and the humanities are also at high risk. In time robotization and new algorithms will be able to accomplish complex cognitive tasks and will threaten the employment of high-skill professionals like radiologists and lawyers. (Frenette and Frank, Summary, pp. 2 and 3) They do throw out a lifeline to some by concluding that new technologies also generate new employment opportunities, both by creating new jobs and by modifying existing ones.

A major sector of any urban economy is sports and culture. In the US, as elsewhere, professional sports are virtually shut down. Baseball is being played in a reduced season of only 60 games, rather than the normal 162. Basketball and hockey are also playing postponed and probably abbreviated seasons, and the National Football League is considering having a normal

season, but when 15 members of the Miami Marlins baseball team came down
with the virus, teams in all leagues had to reconsider their options. Much of this
is still to be determined, but if the shutdown is extensive, estimates are that it
could cost the economy $12 billion in revenues, with teams playing in empty
stadiums, if at all. (AFP) Television viewing and network revenues will also
be significantly reduced.

Throughout the country all theaters, opera performances, recitals and
orchestra concerts have been cancelled, until 2021 in most cases. Some
entities have been giving events on television, performances of members of
the company, or presentations of historic performances. Both performers and
companies have been very active in maintaining contact with their audiences,
albeit at a distance. Seventy-six percent of creative workers have been using
their art to raise morale and to create community cohesion. Ricard Florida and
Michael Seman estimate that through 31 July 2020, the financial losses to the
creative economy, which included film, advertising and fashion as well as
arts and cultural institutions are estimated to have been $150 billion, and 2.7
million jobs. In the arts and cultural sector, the loss will be 1.4 million, or 50
percent, of jobs, and $42.5 billion in revenues. There is a concern, of course,
that many cultural and arts companies and entities will not be able to survive
the loss of revenue for a year and the uncertainty that will burden them in the
near future, so recovery may be rather slow, at best. (Florida and Seman, p. 1)

Both professional sports, and culture and arts institutions are expected to
survive in larger cities since they are crucial elements in the city's brand.
Without either, most city leaders would fear for the future competitiveness and
image of their city. Thus the city governments will try to come up with some
creative financing to keep these entities in operation. The case is not terribly
bad for teams and companies in smaller cities since their financial needs are
not as pressing as they are for the largest entities, such as major museums,
opera companies, and orchestras. There had already been some discussion
of cancelling many minor league teams, even before the impact of the virus
was known. However, the medium-sized cities are the problem – they try to
play baseball, hockey, and other sports with the "big guys" but they lack the
financial base in the community to see these institutions through an extended
financial difficulty. A poll of epidemiologists in June 2020 gave the result that
64 percent of them would not attend a professional sporting event or a cultural
event for at least one year. This will have its impact on the competitive vitality
of many cities, although if all cities are impacted similarly, the competitive
advantage vis à vis other cities will be miniscule.

An issue of considerable importance is the future of globalization and the
notion of a liberal, market economy. Globalization has come under much
criticism in the recent past. The growth of the total pie is evident but the distribution of the pieces has been decidedly skewed toward the top 5 percent of the

income distribution. The issue of income and economic inequality has become perhaps the dominant issue of public policy. The model of a liberal economy and of globalization was corrupted when political processes in the US became dominated by the wealthy who were able to exert pressure, through contributions to legislators to ease regulations that enabled them to operate in an environment with fewer constraints on their behavior so they can increase their incomes, and then to reduce their income taxes so as to enhance their position in relation to other groups in the society. This results in management of the market so that prices could no longer function as indicators of scarcity and abundance and send signals to investors and consumers to act in a rational way. Since the 1970s the real income of the middle- and lower-income groups in US society has had no increase while all of the benefit from increased productivity has been skimmed off by the top 5 percent. With this situation the justification for international trade liberalization deals, coalition building among nations, and the vitality of the international organizations that promote and maintain a world economy of freer trade has been diminished.

The coronavirus experience will only exacerbate these pressures further. Cities have a big stake in the smooth functioning of the global economy. They are the centers of finance, corporate head offices, and produce a significant share of the country's manufactured goods. Restricting the functioning of the global economy will have a significant, negative impact on the economic vitality of cities large and small. In addition to finance and corporate activity, cities are sites of universities and colleges, the functioning of which in the coronavirus world is up for discussion, with many fearing major loss of both revenue and students. They are also hosts to tourism, great and small, and the public will be reluctant to travel and then to lodge, eat and enjoy these places. Airlines, hotels, and restaurants will all suffer significantly when business travel dries up and conferencing by Zoom replaces use of the products of Boeing and Airbus.

C40 Cities is a network of 96 large cities that was established to combat the climate crisis. When the pandemic hit, Los Angeles mayor Eric Garcetti called a meeting of 45 mayors from all parts of the world to assemble to share their experiences and strategies for responding creatively to the new crisis. (Pipa and Bouchet, p. 1) Other groups, such as the United Cities and Local Governments, Global Resilient Cities Network, and the Union of Ibero-American Capital Cities met to design collective actions that would suit individual cities, as well as focused entities such as the Bloomberg Philanthropies Coronavirus Global Response Initiative. It should be noted that Bloomberg is heavily involved in Johns Hopkins University, one of the leading institutions in analyzing and responding to the pandemic. Anthony Pipa and Max Bouchet wrote that "Indeed, the difficulties traditional institutions have faced in providing a coherent and timely response to the pandemic accelerated the impulse for rapid city-to-city cooperation. This instinct was also intensified by the lackluster reaction by many national governments in providing guidance, coordination, and resources within their own countries. Cities and local governments banded together to move forward quickly and decisively". (Pipa and Bouchard, p. 1)

As with most of the consequences of the coronavirus the impact on large cities is uncertain. On the one hand, the disruptions to the housing, office space, and hotel industries can be expected to have very negative consequences. Some urban residents will find the large city to be less inviting as many of its charms have been diminished – fewer, if any, sports events, concerts and other performances, museums etc. are open, bars and restaurants are only partially open, and so forth. Since wealthy predominantly white residents have the mobility to act on their reaction, the large cities may become increasingly minority and lower income. This, at least, is one forecast. On the other hand, overcrowding in large cities may become less of a feature and those who remain may find the new large city at least as inviting as they did the pre-virus city. Shorter lines at a variety of events and venues, less crowding on sidewalks and in parks, and a slower pace of life will be attractive to a large number of current and potential residents, and the "pleasures of urban life" will be, once again, available. Which option is realized is open to discussion and it will be fascinating to see what happens to urban life in the years to come, as the impacts of the coronavirus are finally diminished by successful vaccines.

I think it would be best to end this communication on a positive note. One thing the virus has accomplished in the US is that it made clear to many more Americans what some of the glaring flaws in our society and politics are and the impacts they are having on significant constituencies of the population. The police actions against African Americans have given much new energy to the Black Lives Matter movement and in some cities the protests in the streets are either mixed race in composition or predominantly white. At the same time the virus has thrown into focus the inadequacies of our healthcare system, and the inadequacies of our segregated housing and our education system. Minorities lack access to decent well-paying jobs, public transportation, neighborhood grocery stores with healthy food offerings, and higher education. In Chicago, people who live in high-income neighborhoods have a life expectancy that is 30 years longer than is that of someone living in a poor, Black neighborhood. The list goes on and on. By throwing all of these examples of an inequitable system into public view and opening them to discussion, the virus has aroused in the population a desire to finally work to eradicate their worst effects.

Changes in transportation systems will also benefit city residents through improved access and lower carbon emissions from vehicles. Many cities will begin to experiment with implementation of the "15- or 20-minute city" model that has been introduced in cities such as Paris and Portland, Oregon, in which work, residence, retail and leisure-time venues are all situated within a short walk or bicycle ride. This could be transformative in its impacts.

Rural poverty is a big issue in itself, but the issues presented here are powerfully felt in cities of all sizes, and, as the Editorial Board of the *New York Times* put it: "The pandemic has exacerbated the inequalities of urban life. Lower-income Americans generally unable to work from home are dying at higher rates. And the very idea of abandoning cities is a luxury reserved for those who have the resources to pick up and move. The poor are bound to the places where they are born. The beauty and peril of cities that we are all bound together". The loss of employment of lower income individuals has accompanied the closure of bars, restaurants, and much retail. This has made it clear to the wealthiest residents that their lives are linked inexorably to those who are the poorest – they are all in this together. "The rich need labor; the poor need capital. And the city needs both". (The Editorial Board)

Hence, we now see much discussion of the need to devote more resources to education, housing, and healthcare for all citizens. We need to ensure that all have an acceptable standard of living, be it through higher minimum wage (to increase it from $7.50 to $15.00 per hour) or better access to education and skill development or better conditions of employment, or all of the above. Many cities and states have begun to disallow zoning and other laws that keep wealthy areas limited to single family housing, since apartment buildings are more attractive to lower income and minority families. Head Start is an early education program that has been very important in preparing young students for successful years of education through university – it is available to only 11 percent of eligible children below the age of three and only 36 percent of those aged three to five. Access to programs such as this put one on a track to university, and lack of access consigns one to a job in a fast food chain or to a life of crime and substance abuse.

While the virus will cause hundreds of thousands of city residents to lose their lives, in the longer run the net impacts on the cities and on urban life may actually be positive.

Many foreign travelers, such as Alexis de Tocqueville, have reported that Americans are different to Europeans. We lack many centuries of history and character development that shape European societies and cultures, and that perhaps both sustain them and constrain them in their development. Americans have typically been described as being relatively prone to taking risks and to being less attached to what exists today. Joel Kotkin argues that rather than kings and generals our heroes are entrepreneurs and "disruptive innovators", and he reminds us that: "Many of what became great companies emerged in the Great Depression and subsequent deep recessions". (Kotkin, p. 3) Perhaps this quality will be more powerful than the dismal forecasts of the more pessimistic analysts as we emerge, eventually, from the world of the virus. Certainly, our cities will be the places where all of this gets played out, as they always have been.

REFERENCES

AFP, *Coronavirus US Sport Shutdown will cost $12 Billion: Report*, New York: Agence France Press, 22 July 2020.

Americans for the Arts, "COVID-19's Impact on The Arts, Research & Tracking Update: July 27, 2020", www.AmericansForTheArts.org/node/103614.

Florida, Richard and Michael Seman, "Lost Art: Measuring COVID-19's Devastating Impact on America's Creative Economy", *Bookings Report*, Washington: Brookings, 11 August 2020.

Frenette, Marc and Kristyn Frank, *The Demographics of Automation in Canada: Who Is at Risk?*, Montreal: Institute for Research on Public Policy, 29 June 2020.

Irwin, Neil, "Why Economic Pain Could Persist Even After the Pandemic Is Contained", *New York Times*, 12 May 2020, Section B, Page 1.

Koenig, David, "Boeing CEO says 'New Cutbacks will Take a Toll on Future Employment' as Company Reports a $2.4 billion Second-quarter Loss", *Chicago Tribune*, 29 July 2020, chicagotribune@nsl.chicagotribune.com.

Kotkin, Joel, "How the Virus is Pushing America Toward a Better Future", *Newgeography*, 5 July 2020.

Lakhani, Nina, "End to US Unemployment Protections Could Fuel Wave of Despair and Suicides", *The Guardian*, 13 August 2020, theguardian.com.

Michael, Chris, *Dystopia or Utopia? The Future of Cities could go Either Way*, 2 June 2010, @chrismicaelgdn.

Naud, Daniel and Rémy Tremblay, "Discours sur la qualité de vie et la compétitivité des villes du savoir", in Diane-Gabrielle Tremblay and Rémy Tremblay, (eds), *La Compétitivité Urbaine à l'ère de la Nouvelle Économie*, Québec: Presses de l'Université du Québec, pp. 57–66, 2006.

Pipa, Anthony F. and Max Bouchet, *How to Make the Most of City Diplomacy in the COVID-19 Era*, Brookings, 6 August 2020.

Sanger-Katz, Margot, Claire Cain Miller and Quoctrung Bui, "When 511 Epidemiologists Expect to Fly, Hug and Do 18 Other Everyday Activities Again", *The New York Times*, 8 June 2020, https://nyti.ms/2AfC7R7.

Stiglitz, Joseph, *The Price of Inequality*, New York: W. W. Norton, 2012.

The Editorial Board, "The Cities We Need", *The New York Times*, 11 May 2020.

Thompson, Della, (ed.), *The Oxford Compact English Dictionary*, Oxford: Oxford University Press, 1996.

Index

Achebe, Chinua 58
age distribution
    adults 72–3
    Great Depression (1930) 71
    retired population 73
Alonso, William 93, 96
amenities 9
    climate, effect of 99
    congenial neighborhoods 101–3
    cultural institutions 106–7
    definition 99
    Industrial Triangle 100
    labor categories 101
    migration 21
    municipal transportation 107–8
    New Economic Geography (NEG)
        model 20
    public education 104–5
    public security 108–9
    recreation facilities, access to 105–6
    social services 103–4
    subjective wellbeing (SWB) 99–100
    suitable/quality housing 109–10
    variables 19
architecture 87–8, 96
Art of City-Making, The 24
arts institutions 118
Asheim, Bjørn 101
Ashworth, Gregory 55

bankruptcies 34, 58
Bannerjee, Abhijit 63
Begovic, Boris 91
Bell, Michael 41
Berger, Mark C. 18, 19, 26
best places 22–3
Bezos, Jeff 54
Black Lives Matter movement 7, 120
Blomquist, Glenn C. 18, 19, 26–8
Bloomberg, Michael 90, 119

Bloomberg Philanthropies Coronavirus
    Global Response Initiative 119
Bolsonaro, Jair 115
Borja, Jordi 34, 35, 94
Bouchet, Max 119
Bowling, Ann 18, 26–8
Boyer, R. 19
Bradley, Jennifer 6, 36, 95
Bridson, Kerrie 84
"Broken Windows" approach 85, 95,
    102, 108
Brooks, Rayshard 109
Bruni, Luigino 4
Burnell, James D. 19
Burnham, Daniel 89, 96

Camagni, Roberto 91
Camfield, L. 15
Capello, Roberta 91
Caragliu, Andrea 91
Case, Ann 1, 14, 15, 45, 72, 116
Cassidy, John 63
Castells, Manuel 34, 35, 94
C40 Cities 119
Çevikayak, Gülnur 20
Chihuly, Dale 88
Chinese Exclusion Act (1882) 69
"City Beautiful" 56
city branding 55–6, 65
"City of big Shoulders" 56
"city of the quarter of an hour" concept
    16
city options
    branding 55–6
    gains from economic activity 55
    tech economy 54–5
city rankings 39–40
city size 90–91
    creativity in cities 91
    large city advantages 96
    population 91